C000298703

Doing wh.......

A fresh look at the gifts of the Spirit

Alison Morgan

ReSource

ReSource – helping to build a church which is diverse, local,
renewed in the Spirit and effective in mission

Copyright © Alison Morgan 2009
The right of Alison Morgan to be identified as the author of this work has been asserted by her in accordance with the Copyright, Designs and Patents Act 1988.

All rights reserved. No part of this publication may be reproduced, stored in a retrieval system, or transmitted in any form or by any means, electronic, mechanical, photocopying, recording or otherwise, without the prior written permission of the copyright owner.

Published by:
ReSource
13 Sadler Street, Wells, Somerset BA5 2RR
office@resource-arm.net
www.resource-arm.net
Charity no. 327035

ISBN 978-1-906363-16-1

Unless otherwise stated, all Bible translations are taken from the New Revised Standard Version of the Bible, Anglicized edition, copyright © 1989, 1995 by the Division of Christian Education of the National Council of the Churches of Christ in the United States of America, and are used by permission. All rights reserved.

Scripture on p 8 taken from THE MESSAGE. Copyright © by Eugene Peterson, 1993, 1994, 1995. Used by permission of NavPress Publishing Group.

Photos on pp 43,57 © Alison Morgan
Photo on p 49 © Kim Philpot
Cover image © iStockphoto.com
Images on pp 1,3,811,19,26,27,39,44,62 © iStockphoto.com
Images on pp 4,17,22 ©stockxpert.com
Images on pp 15,29 © The British Library Board
Image on p 56 Liber Scivias Codex 1174, public domain

Printed by Think Ink, 13 Philip Road, Ipswich IP2 8BH

Contents

1. The big picture

2. A new capacity for action

3. The ministry of Jesus

The Gifts of the Spirit

Now concerning spiritual gifts, brothers and sisters, I do not want you to be uninformed... There are varieties of gifts, but the same Spirit; and there are varieties of services, but the same Lord; and there are varieties of activities, but it is the same God who activates all of them in everyone. To each is given the manifestation of the Spirit for the common good. To one is given through the Spirit the utterance of wisdom, and to another the utterance of knowledge according to the same Spirit, to another faith by the same Spirit, to another gifts of healing by the one Spirit, to another the working of miracles, to another prophecy, to another the discernment of spirits, to another various kinds of tongues, to another the interpretation of tongues. All these are activated by one and the same Spirit, who allots to each one individually just as the Spirit chooses.

1 Corinthians 12

The Fruit of the Spirit

By contrast, the fruit of the Spirit is love, joy, peace, patience, kindness, generosity, faithfulness, gentleness, and self-control. There is no law against such things. And those who belong to Christ Jesus have crucified the flesh with its passions and desires. If we live by the Spirit, let us also be guided by the Spirit.

Galatians 5

Part 1 : The Big Picture

*The search for an appropriate spirituality is one of the signs
of our times* – Albert Nolan

Spirituality comes naturally to human beings. Made in the image of
God, created for relationship with him, we are tripartite beings – we
have, as every bookshop owner knows, a mind, a body and also a
spirit. Virtually every human culture throughout history has recognised
this spiritual dimension of our being. From our pre-literate ancestors
at Stonehenge to the mediums of our own day, from the mystery
religions of ancient Greece to the witchdoctors of contemporary
Africa, there has been a constant attempt by people to penetrate
beyond the visible world into the world of the spirit. No human being
is complete unless he or she is to some degree spiritually alive.[1]

The Christian faith offers a coherent and fulfilling way of developing
the spiritual side of our lives through the person of the Holy Spirit. Any
person who places their trust in Jesus may instantly begin to engage
with the Holy Spirit. And yet that's not always as simple as it sounds.
The Holy Spirit is like water – necessary for life, but fast flowing,
shifting constantly in form and focus, powerful. The Holy Spirit is like
wind – exhilarating in the changes it brings, but hard to control, to pin
down, to direct into appropriate channels. The Holy Spirit is like fire –
cleansing, but unpredictable, dangerous. The Spirit brings life, life in all
its fullness – but also has a way of turning things upside down and
inside out, of threatening the status quo. Do we really want spiritual
floods, gales, bush fires sweeping through our lives and across our
lands? It has often seemed that surely we do not.

For the first few centuries after the resurrection of Jesus and the
coming of the Holy Spirit, people all over the known world embraced
the good news that it was now possible for them to engage directly
and personally with God. Groups of active Christian believers sprang
up all over the Roman empire and beyond. Some welcomed the Holy
Spirit with such unbridled enthusiasm that Paul had to write to them
to urge restraint. As the church expanded, organisation became a

pressing need. A hierarchy of leadership was established, and the new leaders sought to impose some kind of order, not just on the people but also, it seems, on the Spirit himself. Imperceptibly the the Church moved gradually further and further from the edgy, dangerous faith of the first Christians, and the wind of the Spirit became indistinguishable from the structures of the Church.[2]

For much of the Church's history since those early days the Spirit has been marginalised.[3] Even when the Spirit is acknowledged he has often been treated, as the Italian theologian Raniero Cantalamessa says, not so much as 'the invisible force permeating all from within' as 'an idea or a theme, which we scatter here and there in our addresses as one would sugar on a pudding.'[4] What began as the sweeping grandeur of a fresh flowing river, a powerful wind, or a forest fire gradually turned into the occasional, carefully authorised, dispensation of bottled water, toy windmills, handheld sparklers.

As the Church, in most places and most of the time, concentrated on the daily necessities of pastoring and teaching its members, erecting its buildings and ordering its finances, new generations of philosophers and scientists taught western societies to focus on the power of human reason rather than on something as nebulous as spirituality. By the 19th century it was possible for Nietzsche to declare that God was dead, and a little while later Lenin suggested that in a world powered by electricy there was no further need for prayer.[5] By the end of the Victorian era church attendance had begun to decline, and people began to look elsewhere for meaning. Perhaps two world wars had knocked people's confidence in God; at any rate the process accelerated in the 50s and 60s. New ideals and aspirations were built by the architects of a new world, and a bright and shiny consumer society set about fulfilling them.

All that sounds discouraging to those of us who continue to place our faith in God; and yet it is not, partly because it's not the whole story, as we shall see, and partly because change is afoot not just in the church but also in the world. Increasingly, not only amongst Christians but especially amongst those outside the Church, there is a dissatisfaction, a lingering question, a hankering after some way of properly expressing that part of our being which is not mind and body but, as the new bookshop shelves proclaim, spirit. We live, Archbishop Rowan Williams suggested recently, 'in a country that is uncomfortably haunted by the memory of religion and doesn't quite know what to do with it.' We need, he said, 'somewhere to put certain bits of our humanity.'[6] The evidence suggests he is right. A BBC poll at the beginning of the new millennium found that 76% of people identify a spiritual dimension to their lives, 38% are aware of the presence of God, and 37% say they have personal experience of answered prayer.[7] Spiritual experimentation of all kinds is rising, neuroscientists researching the activity of the brain are suggesting that spirituality is an undeniable aspect of what it means to be human, and secular writers are publishing books on what is coming to be known as spiritual intelligence.[8]

The difficulty we have is that people who wish to explore the spiritual dimension of life no longer expect to be able to do that in church. 'Are you witches?' asked a young man in amazement as he watched a group of Christians pray effectively for the healing of the sick. A reasonable question, in a country where people are as likely to visit psychic fairs and alternative spiritual practitioners in the search for somewhere to put the homeless 'bits of their humanity' as they are to attend Sunday worship. One vicar told us recently that 30% of his congregation also go to the local spiritualist church. I spoke earlier this year on 'Science and spirituality – has science disproved God?' at a comprehensive school where only a handful of the 1500 students profess any kind of faith. Seventy came, and bombarded me afterwards with a greater variety of searching questions than I have experienced from any adult audience.

Sometimes it's helpful to think about things in picture or story. I recall of the house we used to live in - a comfortable, Victorian house in Leicester. The house was perfect, but we had a problem with the garden. Some time in the 70s developers had bought all the ends of the gardens for a smart new housing estate. There was a stream running across the land. It wasn't a very big one, so they just tarmacked over it and built on top. But one winter the end of our garden began to get soggy. The next winter it was worse; grass turned to moss and moss to standing water. First we planted bog plants, but eventually we decided the only solution was to dig a channel from one side of the garden to the other, and recreate the stream. You can't tarmac over running water; it has a way of bursting out somewhere else. It's the same with the living water of the Spirit – try as we may, the spiritual dimension to our lives cannot be easily suppressed.[9]

Somewhat to the surprise of the architects, the new houses built over the stream at the end of our garden no longer look so new. Their windows are small, the roofing materials shoddy, the fences leaning. People are not so keen to live there as once they were. And so it is too with our new, spiritless world; somehow it fails to deliver. Journalist Clifford Longley puts it well:

'Having constructed a society of unprecedented sophistication, convenience and prosperity, nobody can remember what it was supposed to be for. Just enjoying it does not seem to be enough. Indeed enjoyment as an end in itself quickly turns to ashes in the mouth. Not only is it boringly bland. It is even more boringly purposeless. There is more to human life than comfort, entertainment and the avoidance of suffering.'[10]

We live in a comfortable but dry and flattened world. A world, it's been suggested, without windows. A world which for all its comforts and opportunities is relationship poor and spiritually stunted. A world in which people have many questions, and few satisfactory answers. How can we help?

Embracing authentic spirituality

Jesus cried out, "If anyone thirsts, let him come to me and drink. Rivers of living water will brim and spill out of the depths of anyone who believes in me in this way, just as the Scripture says". (He said this in regard to the Spirit, whom those who believed in him were about to receive).   John 7.37-39, The Message.

When the Bible talks about spirituality, it has none of the nebulous experimentality of our faltering contemporary use of the word. Spirituality in scripture is not a yearning or a dimension, it's a person: the person of the Holy Spirit. 'Do nothing', Jesus told his followers, 'until the Holy Spirit has come upon you. Then you will receive power, and you will be my witnesses to the ends of the earth.' Within days the Spirit came; and those nervous followers found that their lives, and the lives of those with whom they spoke and prayed, had changed forever. The new 'Way' of being and living had an enormous impact; it's been estimated that the Christian church grew by 40% per decade throughout the first few centuries, just by the adding of one startled person at a time.[11]

Dutch theologian Hendrikus Berkhof once wrote that 'to a great extent, official church history is the story of the *defeats* of the Spirit'.[12] And yet during the last hundred years that has not been so. From the beginning of the 20th century there has been, in many places, a new willingness to be open to the Holy Spirit. It led to an equally startled wave of human response all over the world. There are now over 500 million 'charismatic' Christians worldwide, making up some 27% of the total number of church members. Their numbers continue even today to grow by an average of 3% per year.[13] What are they looking for? Not, as has been justly remarked, for answers to intellectual questions, but for a transforming relationship with God; for somewhere to put the bits of their humanity which are not satisfied by the mundane; for somewhere to live, not just materially but emotionally and spiritually. In a nutshell, for something that works. [14]

The Holy Spirit is not an easy person to understand. Gregory of Nazianzus called him 'the God whom nobody writes about'. He's been called the orphan of theology and yet the stealth weapon of the Church.[15] When Jesus spoke about the Holy Spirit he spoke about him, quite simply, as a person: someone who was to come, someone who would teach, guide, counsel, comfort, encourage and work in and through those who welcomed him.[16] Within a few years Paul was writing about him in a slightly different way - a way which did not promise what was to come so much as describe what was already happening. The Holy Spirit, Paul explained, is recognised and experienced in two main ways: he brings 'gifts', and he brings 'fruit'.[17] The 'gifts' enable us to relate to other people in a way that transcends our own human limitations, to do the things that Jesus did. They are best seen not as a set of new possessions so much as a new capacity for action, given to us not for our own benefit but for that of others. The 'fruit' of the Spirit, on the other hand, is recognised not through the things that we do but in the things we become: a person who has received the Holy Spirit gradually changes on the inside, until his or her emotional makeup is characterised by love, joy, peace, patience, kindness, generosity, faithfulness, gentleness, and self-control.

This is the sales pitch of the kingdom of God: count your cash, said Jesus, calculate the cost, and sign up. It may be demanding; but it's the only way to be authentically human.[18] Authentic spirituality is a God-given spirituality which enables those who receive it to both live and act in a new, more powerful and more fulfilling way.

> Spiritual renewal is about turning to God and seeking for hidden treasure, for the resources that he provides to enable us to respond appropriately to what he is saying and doing today – Josephine Bax

Becoming 'culturally charismatic'?

The fruit of the Spirit is grown carefully, usually over time, through obedience and often through pain. It comes from the careful, coaching companionship of the Holy Spirit who walks with us on our life journey, helping us to grow into the likeness of Christ. The gifts, on the other hand, can be sought and deployed here and now, and often have been. In this country many individuals and churches were transformed by a reawakened openness to the gifts of the Spirit during the 70s and 80s. The effects of this most recent rediscovery cannot be underestimated, and although overall church membership has continued to decline, the church has in many ways become healthier and more vibrant as a result. The UK has become, as Bishop Graham Cray has remarked, a net exporter of spiritual renewal.

And yet all is not as well as it could be. Our age profile, for a start. Whilst thousands of young people gather each year at the Soul Survivor and Momentum events in Somerset, they come from a tiny minority of mostly urban churches, and represent a fraction of their generation. Then there's our sense of purpose. It seems that many churches which embraced the new move of the Spirit thirty or more years ago are now finding their initial enthusiasm has dimmed, as if the excitement of watching God at work has somehow turned into a wondering question – what was it all about, what was it for? And then there's the problem of the inevitable cultural packaging which seems to drape itself imperceptibly around any new initiative. Many churches, not caught up in the initial wave of rediscovery, are now moving towards it, but with a note of caution. 'We want more of the Holy Spirit, we want to come into the things of the Spirit', church leaders often say to us; 'but we don't want to become culturally charismatic' (or words to that effect) – by which they mean that they do want to open their church more fully to the Holy Spirit, but feel hesitant about embracing certain features commonly associated with the charismatic movement. Guitars are not listed among the gifts of the Spirit!

This book is written, 30 years after the first books on the gifts of the Spirit began to tumble out of publishing houses, in the conviction that it's only through growing the fruit and exercising the gifts of the Holy Spirit, in context dependent ways, that we will enable our generation to connect with God. And it's written too in the hope that if, after thirty years and more of renewed experience of the Holy Spirit, we can somehow stand back and look at the bigger picture, we will be able to integrate what we have learned into our normal, Christ-centred lives,

and move on better equipped to minister to a confused and thirsty world.

> The Holy Spirit is given so we can be in a measure what Jesus himself was, part of God's future arriving in the present. The Holy Spirit comes from the world that is waiting to be born – Tom Wright

Looking back through history

Although we are witnessing an unprecedented rediscovery of the life available to us through the Spirit, the gifts of the Spirit have been exercised, often on the margins of the Church, throughout history. They are not the ecclesiastical equivalent of the drugs so enthusiastically embraced by many in the 60s, to be grown out of as we move on into less heady times. They are not the property of a particular subcultural grouping within the Church, to be exercised on Sundays by specially anointed people to the accompaniment of guitars. The gifts of the Spirit have been part of the experience of the normal Christian life for two thousand years. We have contemporary written accounts of healings and deliverances, miracles, prophecy, words of knowledge, discernment and tongues from virtually every century since apostolic times.

This is the story of the healing of a girl through the prayers of Martin of Tours in the 4th century. It was written by Martin's friend and disciple Sulpicius Severus:

A certain girl at Treves was so completely prostrated by a terrible paralysis that for a long time she had been quite unable to make use of her body for any purpose and, being as it were already dead, only the smallest breath of life seemed still to remain in her. Her afflicted relatives were standing by expecting nothing but her death when it was suddenly announced that Martin had come to that city. When the father of the girl found that such was the case he ran to make a request on behalf of his all but lifeless child. It happened that Martin had already entered the church . There, while the people were looking on, and in the presence of many other bishops, the old man uttering a cry of grief embraced the saint's knees and said 'My

12

daughter is dying of a miserable kind of infirmity; and what is more dreadful than death itself she is now alive only in the spirit, her flesh being already dead before the time. I beseech thee to go to her and give her thy blessing; for I believe that through you she will be restored to health'. Martin, troubled by such an address, was bewildered and shrank back saying that this was a matter not in his own hands; that the old man was mistaken in the judgment he had formed and that he was not worthy to be the instrument through whom the Lord should make a display of his power. The father, in tears, persevered in still more earnestly pressing the case. At last, constrained by the bishops standing by to go as requested, he went down to the home of the girl. An immense crowd was waiting at the doors to see what the servant of the Lord would do. And first, betaking himself to his familiar arms in affairs of that kind, he cast himself down on the ground and prayed. Then gazing earnestly upon the ailing girl he requested that oil should be given him. After he had received and blessed this he poured the powerful sacred liquid into the mouth of the girl and immediately her voice returned to her. Then gradually through contact with him her limbs began, one by one, to recover life till at last, in the presence of the people, she arose with firm steps. [19]

It's a good story, and being contemporary with the events themselves not easily dismissed as an idealised biography. Sulpicius writes in his preface: 'I implore those who are to read what follows to give full faith to the things narrated, and to believe that I have written nothing of which I had not certain knowledge and evidence. I should, in fact, have preferred to be silent rather than to narrate things which are false.' It's one of many surviving similar accounts – some are listed on page 14. [20]

The gifts of tongues and interpretation are often assumed to be a relatively recent rediscovery. In fact, the gift of tongues was exercised not only throughout the early Christian centuries but also, for example, by Francis of Assisi in the 13th and Ignatius of Loyola in the 16th, and by many during the Welsh Revival in the early 20th century. But my favourite account comes in the autobiography dictated by a remarkable illiterate housewife from King's Lynn in the early 15th century. Margery Kempe does not use the biblical terminology of tongues, but she does tell how when on pilgrimage to Rome she prayed that a particular priest in the church of St John Lateran, a German, would be able to hear her confession, she and he having no common language. Communicating through an interpreter, they covenanted to pray for divine assistance in this matter. She writes:

After thirteen days the priest came back to her to test the effect of their prayers, and then he understood what she said in English to him, and she understood what he said. And yet he did not understand the English that other people spoke; even though they spoke the same words that she spoke, he still did not understand them unless she spoke herself. Then she was confessed to this priest of all her sins, as near as her memory would serve her, from her childhood up until that hour, and received her penance very joyfully.

Perhaps not surprisingly, this story was doubted by those who heard it. Some decided to put it to the test:

Her confessor was asked to dinner and, when the time came, was seated and served with this good priest and his party - the said creature being present - and the good English priest chatting and conversing in their own language, English. The German priest, a worthy cleric as is written before, confessor to the said creature, sat quietly in a sort of gloom, because he did not understand what they said in English, but only when they spoke Latin. And they did it on purpose, unbeknown to him, to prove whether he understood English or not. At last, the said creature - seeing and well understanding that her confessor did not understand their language, and that it was tedious to him - partly to cheer him up and partly, or much more, to prove the work of God, told him in her own language, in English, a story of Holy Writ, which she had learned from clerics while she was at home in England, for she would not talk of any vanity or fantasies. Then they asked her confessor if he understood what she had said, and he straightaway in Latin told them the same words that she said before in English, for he could neither speak English nor understand English except from her tongue. And then they were astonished, for they knew that he understood what she said, and she understood what he said, and yet he could not understand any other English person. So blessed may God be, who made a foreigner to understand her when her own countrymen had abandoned her, and would not hear her confession unless she would leave off her weeping and talking of holiness.[21]

There are heart-warming accounts of miracles and deliverances from many different periods, but here's a slightly more alarming example of prophecy, from the life of the 17th century Scottish Reformer John Welsh:

One night at supper, he was speaking of the Lord and his Word to all who were sitting at the table. Everyone at the table was being edified by Welsh's conversation with the exception of one young man who laughed and sometimes mocked him. Welsh endured this for a while, but then abruptly stopped in the middle of his discourse. A sad look came over Welsh's face, and he told everyone at the dinner table to be silent "and observe the work of the Lord upon that mocker." Immediately, the young man sank beneath the table and died.[22]

St Guthlac casts out a demon, from a 13th century English manuscript.
Copyright © British Library Board, Harley Roll Y6, roundel 10.

	The Gifts of the Spirit in History
Century	Testimonies of the exercising of the gifts are recorded from the lives and in the writings of the following:
1	The Didache, Shepherd of Hermas
2	Quadratus, Justin Martyr, Irenaeus, Clement of Rome, the Montanists
3	Origen, Tertullian, Novatian, Gregory the wonderworker, Hyppolytus, Cyprian, Ignatius of Antioch, Clement of Alexandria, Athanasius
4	Antony, Hilarion, Macrina, Ambrose, St Martin of Tours, Eusebius, Cyril of Jerusalem, Antony, Basil, Gregory of Nazianzus, Hilary of Poitiers, Basil of Caesarea, Epiphanius of Salamis
5	Augustine
6	Gregory of Tours, Gregory the Great, Joseph Hazaya of Syria
7-8	Bede – Cuthbert, John of Beverley, Aidan
10	Ulrich of Augsburg
11	Anselm
12	Bernard, Richard of St Victor, Hildegard of Bingen, Hugh of Lincoln, William of Malmesbury
13	Francis, Bonaventure, Thomas Aquinas, Gertrude of Helfta
14-15	Vincent Ferrer, Margery Kempe, Brigitta of Sweden, Catherine of Siena, Gregory Palamas, Colette of Corbi
16	Martin Luther, Ignatius Loyola, Teresa of Avila, George Wishart, John Knox, the Huguenots
17	Valentine Greatlakes, John Welch, Richard Baxter, Robert Bruce, Alexander Peden, George Fox, the Quakers
18	John Wesley, Count Zinzendorf, Thomas Munster, Seraphim of Sarov, the Jansenists
19	JC Blumhardt, Curé d'Ars, Charles Spurgeon, Edward Irving, Charles Cullis, Maria Woodworth-Etter, Lourdes

In the process of the continual reformation in the life of the Church, Christians move on not through original and new ideas, but through rediscovering and refreshing our understanding of different aspects of our tradition which have become lost or neglected in a particular context – Steven Croft

Spiritual gifts today

On the first evening after his resurrection, Jesus came to the disciples and said 'Peace be with you. As the Father has sent me, so I send you.' When he had said this, he breathed on them and said to them, 'Receive the Holy Spirit'. John 20.20-21

The excitement which accompanied our own rediscovery of the gifts of the Spirit has often led us to forget why and how they are given. It seems as if often they have become ends in themselves, provided in order to bring a frisson of faith-enhancing excitement to those who receive and exercise them. Some of those who have not been part of this experience have felt marginalised – most notoriously with regard to the gift of tongues, still hailed by many as a universal mark of the presence of the Holy Spirit in an individual. Others have wondered why it is that the single chapter of 1 Corinthians 12 seems to have shot to the head of the scriptural Top Ten, at the expense of not just those passages which describe the fruit of the Spirit but even at that of the gospels themselves. Others just wish the gifts of the Spirit were part of their own daily experience, but are unsure where to begin.

Perhaps it's helpful to remember that there is nothing especially remarkable about 1 Corinthians 12 except this: it describes the ministry of Jesus. Jesus' charismatic ministry began after his baptism and the coming upon him of the Holy Spirit; it was at that point that he ceased to be a carpenter and began to minister with wisdom and knowledge, healing the sick and curing those troubled with unclean spirits, exercising discernment, prophesying and living by faith whatever the circumstances.[23] He told his disciples that they too

would work as he had worked, and that this would be made possible through the same Holy Spirit, who would come to them in their turn after his death. He specifically told them to do nothing until that had happened. At that point, he said, they would begin a life of witness to him, doing the things that he had done, guided and equipped in everything by the Spirit.[24]

So the Holy Spirit and his gifts are given to us so that we might play our part in the continued mission and ministry of Jesus. They are given, as Tom Wright has remarked, not to provide us with the spiritual equivalent of a trip to Alton Towers, but so that we might take the victory of the cross into the world.[25] They are the tools of our trade; the tools of mission.

This is confirmed by a simple study of the gospels, summarised in Part 3 of this book. In each of Luke and John it is possible to identify 80 instances of the use of a gift or gifts of the Spirit as described by Paul in 1 Corinthians 12, mostly by Jesus. There areanother 66 instances in the Book of Acts. It would seem that without the gifts of the Spirit we have neither the right nor the power to minister the gospel. This is Puritan theologian John Owen, not beating about the bush:

'Nothing at all can be done without these spiritual gifts, and therefore a ministry devoid of them is a mock ministry, and no ordinance of Christ... To erect a ministry by virtue of outward order, rites, and ceremonies, without gifts for the edification of the church, is but to hew a block with axes, and smooth it with planes, and set it up for an image to be adored. To make a man a minister who can do nothing of the proper peculiar work of the ministry, nothing towards the only end of it in the church, is to set up a dead carcass, fastening it to a post, and expecting it should do you work and service.'[26]

So if it is the fruit of the Spirit that we should desire for ourselves, for our own growth and benefit, it's the gifts that we should desire in order to enable us to reach out to others. If we minister in our own strength we do not minister at all.

Jesus, filled with the power of the Spirit, returned to Galilee, and a report about him spread through all the surrounding country. He began to teach in their synagogues and was praised by everyone. When he came to Nazareth, where he had been brought up, he went to the synagogue on the sabbath day, as was his custom. He stood up to read, and the scroll of the prophet Isaiah was given to him. He unrolled the scroll and found the place where it was written:

"The Spirit of the Lord is upon me, because he has anointed me to bring good news to the poor. He has sent me to proclaim release to the captives and recovery of sight to the blind, to let the oppressed go free, to proclaim the year of the Lord's favour."

And he rolled up the scroll, gave it back to the attendant, and sat down. The eyes of all in the synagogue were fixed on him. Then he began to say to them, "Today this scripture has been fulfilled in your hearing."

Luke chapter 4

Exercising the gifts in love

We are English, and we like to impose order on our experience. The Romans did too, and perhaps it's not for nothing that both the Romans and the British ended up running empires. But the Greeks were different, and it's no surprise that it was to the new Christian believers in the vibrant and cosmopolitan city of Corinth that Paul found himself writing about the gifts of the Spirit. Famous for its wealth, its Games, its crafts, its temple to Aphrodite and its love of luxurious and sensuous living, Corinth was not a cautious place. The new Christians had embraced the gifts of the Spirit with apparently unbridled enthusiasm, and Paul wrote to them to urge restraint and remind them that God is a God not of chaos but of order. We are indebted to them, for it is from their excesses that we get our clearest description of what the new, Spirit dependent life was meant to look like.

Paul makes a number of points. Firstly, the gifts of the Spirit are given to the body of Christian believers as a whole. That is, they are not intended as feathers in the cap of individuals but as spiritual resources given to enable the mission and ministry of the church. This makes sense: John says that Jesus himself was given the Spirit 'without measure' (John 3.34), whereas Paul reminds us that to each of us the Spirit is given 'according to the measure' of Christ's gift (Ephesians 4.7). In other words, the complete range of the Spirit's gifting resided in Jesus, but for us it's shared among his whole body, the church. This is made clear in both 1 Corinthians 12 and Romans 12. We are all given different gifts.

The gifts of the Spirit seem to be given in two main contexts. Firstly, in the context Jesus himself received them – that is, as we go about our business as his representative in the world in which we live. Jesus was given prophetic insight into the lives of those he met in his travels, and the power to heal and deliver the sick. The gifts are the tools of mission, given as signs of the kingdom to those who as yet have not had the opportunity to enter it. This is the experience of many Christians today, especially those who exercise the ministry of an evangelist. John Wimber, for example, tells the well known story of how he saw the word 'adultery' written over the forehead of a fellow passenger on an aeroplane.[27] We may be impelled to initiate a conversation with someone, or be overcome with a sense of the presence of evil as we enter a particular environment, or emboldened to pray for a specific outcome in a certain circumstance. These are all the marks of the Spirit at work in and through us.

But the gifts are also exercised when we wait on God together. So we find that people seem to be more readily healed when we pray for them in the context of a communion service. People seem to receive the gifts of tongues and interpretation more easily during a time of corporate prayer or praise. Prophetic words come most often when we meet together. It goes against our individualistic culture – but that's how it seems to be.

In either event, whether we are working alone or meeting together, the metaphors we are given to help us understand how the Spirit works are all collective ones – the body, the vine: radically different from the more contemporary and alluring ones of the celebrity, the star. It's an important point – many high profile charismatic leaders have lost their way by thinking of themselves not as ordinary members of the body of Christ, but as ministers who enjoy a more special anointing than those they serve. I once attended a meeting led by an Argentinian pastor, a gifted man with a wonderful testimony of healing. After he had spoken, he encouraged people to come forward to receive the touch of the Holy Spirit with the words: 'there is blessing in my hands'. Hm, I thought. They were all duly touched by the faithful Spirit; but within a year the pastor had been sacked for financial irregularities. In this as in all else, humility is the key to success. Karl Barth observed long ago that our major concern should not be with the phenomena themselves or with the person through whom they occur, but with what they point to, and who they bear witness to. It's not us on the stage.[28]

Paul's discussion of spiritual gifts in 1 Corinthians falls into two parts. The first is chapter 12, where he emphasizes that we are all given not the same but different gifts, and that we should use them in an orderly and servant hearted way. The second is chapter 14, where he speaks in more detail about the need for coherence and interpretation, and

21

about the importance of prophecy over and above tongues. It seems that the Corinthians had all been hopping up and down in a frenzy of tongues, all at the same time – very likely modelling themselves on the pagan oracles, where prophetesses often spoke in an ecstatic trance which then had to be interpreted by their attendants.

What comes in between these two chapters is 1 Corinthians 13, and it is here that Paul makes his second major point: the gifts of the Spirit are to be exercised in love, and the love - itself a fruit of the Spirit - is more important than the gifts. It is no accident that chapter 13 comes between chapters 12 and 14 - Paul was writing not with an eye to future wedding services but in order to make a specific point about the use of the spiritual gifts when Christians meet together. The principle is not me but you: it's love. We find the same link between effective ministry and love in John 15, where Jesus uses the image of the vine to suggest that it is through living in loving obedience to the Spirit and commitment to one another that we become fruitful. Without the guiding and restraining influence of love we will experience only chaos and confusion. It's worth noting that theologians since the time of Augustine have recognised the Spirit as the gift of love which unites the Father with the Son, and the Son with us - not the kind of love known to the thousand alluring priestesses of Aphrodite and their Corinthian clients, but the kind of love which subordinates ourselves to Jesus and, through him, to others. [29]

If I speak in the tongues of mortals and of angels, but do not have love, I am a noisy gong or a clanging cymbal. And if I have prophetic powers, and understand all mysteries and all knowledge, and if I have all faith, so as to remove mountains, but do not have love, I am nothing. 1 Cor. 13.1

The words and what they mean

Paul talks about spiritual gifts not just in his letter to the Corinthians but also in those he wrote to the Romans and Ephesians, and it is tempting to place these texts alongside one another to see if we can draw up a systematic list of gifts, perhaps adding one or two from other parts of the New Testament.[30] The difficulty with such an approach is that although there is a definite overlap there are also clear differences between the three passages. These are sometimes resolved by attempting to distinguish between gifts given by God (Rome), by Jesus (Ephesus), or by the Spirit (Corinth); or between motivational, leadership, and spiritual gifts – there is support in the text for all these points of view. Other commentators simply add the whole lot together and list up to 28 different gifts without regard for the context in which they are described.[31]

Maybe we are moving into an age when it seems less important for everything to slot cog-like into everything else; maybe we are getting better at tolerating ambiguity – or perhaps just recognising that the New Testament is a set of messages written not as a tidy manual but as a series of words directed into specific contexts, and that this has an impact on how they are received not just then but also now. Whether that's right or not, there do seem to be a number of things which it is helpful to bear in mind when thinking about gifts, all of which warn us not to be too simplistic in our reading of these passages.

1. Language

Most of us read the New Testament in translation. The English translations of the passages in Romans 12, Ephesians 4 and 1 Corinthians 12 all use the same word 'gifts' – but the original Greek does not. When writing to the Romans and Corinthians Paul uses the word *charismata* ('expressions of grace'), but in his letter to the Ephesians he also uses the word *doreas* (from which we get our word 'dowry').[32] And not only does he choose a different word, he uses it in a different way. Whereas to the Corinthians he says that we receive spiritual gifts which he then goes on to describe, to the Ephesians he says that the gifts that Christ gave were 'that some would be apostles, some prophets, some evangelists, some pastors and teachers, to equip the saints for the work of ministry'. That is, it is the people appointed to the offices of apostle, evangelist, prophet, pastor and teacher who are given as gifts to the church. They don't receive these offices as gifts; they are themselves given.

Secondly, even in his letter to the Corinthians Paul does not use a single word 'gift' as we find in English. Indeed he does not speak, literally, about 'gifts of the Spirit' at all. Within the space of seven verses he uses a whole series of different words: spiritual things (*pneumatika*, 12.1, 14.1), graces (*charismata*, 12.4, 12.31), ministries or services (*diakonion* 12.5), working or activities or energisings (*energematon*, 12.6, 12.11) and manifestations (*phanerosis*, 12.7). The common element to them all is not so much what it's like to receive them as who it is who gives them – the Holy Spirit. In English we simply read 'gift', which represents a translator's attempt to convey meaning ('thing given') rather than a literal word for word exchange. As ever, things can get lost in translation: having read 'gift', we turn it mentally into 'present'; and then it's only a short step to thinking about ourselves and what's in it for me – thus changing the whole emphasis of the passage. This is a textbook lesson in oversimplification.

> In Greek the words grace and gift of grace (*charis*, *charismata*) are related to the word for joy (*chara*).

2. Context

Paul was famously anxious to match his presentations to his audiences. Earlier in his letter to the Corinthians he had explained that he tries to be a Jew to Jews, law-abiding to the law-abiding, free to the free, weak to the weak; he becomes all things to all people, so that he might save some.[33] So in matters of dress, behaviour, and language, Paul attempts to fit himself to the customs of his audience. He wants them to notice not his speech or background, but his relationship with God. It's an important principle for anyone who works outside their own culture; I know not only that I communicate better in Italy if I use my hands and raise my voice, and in Africa if I wear a skirt and move my feet when I sing, but also that words and phrases are not just one on one codes to crack but carry within their nuances a whole different way of thinking and being. Language is not a code, but the expression of a set of experiences. Paul knew this too, and it's important to bear it in mind when we come to read his discussion of the gifts of the Spirit.

The Corinthians were not, as we've already, seen, coming from nowhere as far as spiritual things were concerned. The city of Corinth was alive with spiritual beliefs and practices of all kinds, so much so that their influence was creeping into the church – which is why Paul begins this section of his letter by reminding them that they are no longer subject to idols, and that the spirit within them now is the Spirit of God. But it's striking, as he goes on, that many of the words he uses in his discussion of the gifts of the Spirit will have been very familiar to the Corinthians. They carried associations for them which they do not for us; and this may account for the difficulty the more cautious commentators experience in pinning down their precise meaning. Wisdom and knowledge in particular need to be viewed not in the light of a modern, rational way of thinking but against a background of esoteric gnostic philosophies and the cults of pagan mystery religions; and Paul will have had that in mind when he chose them. Indeed, he's already spent some time on both earlier in the letter. It's another reason to be careful before we assume this is a context-free discussion of eternal realities.

3. Purpose

There is an intriguing discrepancy not just between Paul's various letters, but even within this single chapter of 1 Corinthians 12, and this too suggests that Paul probably did not intend to offer an analytical discussion of a number of clear cut and well defined gifts. At the beginning of the chapter he lists the nine gifts which we will look at in Part 2. But there's another discussion at the end of the chapter which overlaps with the earlier one but is substantially different from it. This second bite at the cherry seems to offer a hotchpotch of roles and gifts, then throws in a few extra and noticeably unspectacular things for good measure – helps and 'governings', often translated as administration or 'strategic insight'. It would seem that Paul was choosing his earlier words in relation to the specific situation in Corinth, and that he now completes the discussion out by pointing out that those rather spectacular, spontaneous gifts represent only a small part of the work of the Spirit. His main aim is to demonstrate the diversity of the Spirit's workings rather than to offer precise definitions of clearly delineated gifts.[34]

Living in expectation

How then are we to read 1 Corinthians 12? It's worth bearing in mind something John Wimber once said: that the Bible is meant to be the menu, and so often we treat it as if it were the meal, as if the written marks on the page were themselves the reality that in fact they only point to. Just imagine, he says, going into a restaurant and settling down at your table. The waiter brings the menu. You pore over it. Mm, yes, look. Roast duck in orange sauce. Pan-fried baby squid with wild mushrooms and peppers. Lemon syllabub. Fresh raspberry tart. Mmm... You spend a happy half hour or so browsing, savouring the various possibilities. Then you stand up, hand the menu back to the waiter with a smile of thanks, and leave. Often, he says, that's what we do with the Bible. We read it, admire it, and close it. We don't actually expect anything to happen. This is a salutary warning. It's not careful, theological study of the gifts of the Spirit which will advance the kingdom of God; it's trying to use them. We do need to pay close attention to the menu - but we mustn't mistake it for the meal.[35]

How can we escape if we neglect so great a salvation? It was declared at first through the Lord and it was attested to us by those who heard him, while God added his testimony by signs and wonders and various miracles, and by gifts of the Holy Spirit, distributed according to his will.
Hebrews 2.3-4

Part 2 : A new capacity for action

Do not get drunk with wine, but [keep on being] filled with the Spirit.
Ephesians 5.18

Understanding 1 Corinthians 12

One of the ways in which Paul talks about the 'gifts' of the Spirit is to say that they are 'charisms', or expressions of grace (vs 4). He refers to them in his introduction as 'energisings' which operate through people but depend on the energy which comes from God (vs 6); and he summarises his initial discussion by saying that all of the gifts derive their energy from the Spirit (vs 11). So two things are true: the gifts are unmerited and freely given; and they are given so that God can *do* something – energy is power, a force which brings about change.

It's been said, therefore, that the gifts of the Spirit are not so much a new property as a new capacity for action.[36] They are not a party bag but rather a toolkit; the power tools available to us as we live and minister in the name of Jesus. They are an outflowing of divine energy, made available to operate through human vessels as they are needed. It follows that they are not to be seen as possessions, but rather as manifestations of the Spirit which come in the context of active prayer and ministry. So although we may find that we often receive a particular gift as we minister, we do not say that we 'have' the gift of wisdom or knowledge or healing, only that we often find God working through us in this way. Each time we exercise a gift we do so under a fresh enabling of the Spirit.[37]

Many people have written about their extraordinary experiences of the Holy Spirit at work. Although it is tempting to draw upon such stories, I have deliberately chosen to use only 'ordinary' examples of the gifts of the Spirit in action – examples drawn from my own experience or offered to me directly by

27

others. In so doing I hope to emphasize that the Spirit is active not just in the ministry of anointed leaders in faraway places, but also through the daily lives of ordinary Christian believers here in Britain.

A word of wisdom

'To one through the Spirit is given a word of wisdom', Paul begins. The nature of wisdom seems to have been a bit of a hot potato in Corinth, and Paul has already tried at some length to ensure that his hearers have a godly and not a pagan understanding of what it is. It is not, he has said, the kind of wisdom sought by the Greeks, but that which God has chosen to reveal in Christ; and it is not accessed through human experience but taught by the Spirit. Wisdom, he says, is 'knowing the mind of Christ' – it's about knowing how to live in a world in which the foundational event is the cross.[38] James suggests that spiritual wisdom is something every Christian should ask for, and remarks that the life of a person in whom it is present will be marked by purity, peace, mercy and other good fruits. [39]

Wisdom in this sense requires neither intellectual complexity nor human judgment, which makes it rather different not only from the default Corinthian assumptions about it but also from our own understanding. It does however put it firmly in the context of the wisdom teaching of the Old Testament, where Wisdom is represented as the companion of God, intimately involved in creation and present to help all those who seek her to live in harmony with eternal reality.[40]

The spiritual nature of wisdom is confirmed by a study of those who are said to have been granted it. In the Old Testament, Joshua is said to have been full of the spirit of wisdom after Moses laid hands on him. Joseph is recognised by Pharoah to be full of the spirit of God, discerning and wise, following his dream interpretation. Solomon prayed for wisdom and is known to this day for his wise judgments and writings. And Isaiah foretold that the spirit of the Lord, the spirit of wisdom, understanding, counsel and might would rest on the Messiah.[41]

A word of wisdom

<u>Solomon orders a DNA test...</u>

Two women who were prostitutes came to the king and stood before him. The one woman said, 'Please, my lord, this woman and I live in the same house; and I gave birth while she was in the house. Then on the third day after I gave birth, this woman also gave birth. We were together; there was no one else with us in the house, only the two of us were in the house. Then this woman's son died in the night, because she lay on him. She got up in the middle of the night and took my son from beside me while your servant slept. She laid him at her breast, and laid her dead son at my breast. When I rose in the morning to nurse my son, I saw that he was dead; but when I looked at him closely in the morning, clearly it was not the son I had borne.' But the other woman said, 'No, the living son is mine, and the dead son is yours.' The first said, 'No, the dead son is yours, and the living son is mine.' So they argued before the king. Then the king said, 'The one says, "This is my son that is alive, and your son is dead", while the other says, "Not so! Your son is dead, and my son is the living one".' So the king said, 'Bring me a sword,' and they brought a sword before the king. The kind said, 'Divide the living boy in two; then give half to the one, and half to the other.' But the woman whose son was alive said to the king – because compassion for her son burned within her – 'Please, my lord, give her the living boy; certainly do not kill him!' The other said, 'It shall be neither mine nor yours; divide it.' Then the king responded: 'Give the first woman the living boy; do not kill him. She is his mother.' All Israel heard of the judgment that the king had rendered; and they stood in awe of the king, because they perceived that the wisdom of God was in him, to execute justice.

1 Kings 3.16-28

The Judgment of Solomon, from a 14th century French Bible
© British Library Board, Royal 19 C. II, f.273

If spiritual gifts characterise the ministry of Jesus it seems natural to look to Jesus for examples of their use. Luke tells us that right from the beginning people were astonished at the authority with which he spoke.As the gospels unfold we see him responding time and again with wisdom to all manner of issues and questions: Why do you eat with tax collectors and sinners? Do you drive out demons by demonic power? Why do your disciples not wash their hands before they eat? Should Jews pay taxes to Caesar? What should be done with this woman found committing adultery? In all cases the answer Jesus gives to these life questions is theological – that is, it's an answer which derives from the nature of the kingdom of God, and not from law or custom. 'Where did this man get this wisdom and these deeds of power?' people wonder in Nazareth; 'is this not the carpenter's son?'. It makes no worldly sense.[42]

The same kind of wisdom begins to operate in his disciples after Jesus's death. He had promised that when brought to trial, they would be given the wisdom to know how to answer the accusations made against them, and we see this happening straight away.[43] We also see them tackling one dilemma after another in a godly manner or, as we might say today, according to kingdom values – the appointment of wise, Spirit filled men to help with food distribution, the decision not to require non-Jewish Christians to be circumcised, and Peter's own understanding through a dream that he was to share the gospel with the Gentile centurion Cornelius. Peter himself says that Paul's letters are written 'according to the wisdom given him'.[44]

So it would seem that a word of wisdom is one which enables us to live in harmony with God's plans and purposes in a given situation, and in particular with the message of Christ crucified. It might come as a word of guidance or encouragement at a difficult moment, as a word preached or understanding received through prayer, or as godly and helpful answers provided to complex and challenging questions.

I pray that the God of our Lord Jesus Christ may give you a spirit of wisdom and revelation so that, with the eyes of your heart enlightened, you may know what is the hope to which he has called you, what are the riches of his glorious inheritance, and what is the immeasurable greatness of his power for us who believe.   Ephesians 1.17-19

Wisdom today

Wisdom in resolving conflict

Our church once went through a time of great conflict and turmoil, and in a public meeting chaired by the bishop a woman named Kathleen, who occupied no leadership position, stood up, read a rebuke from scripture, spoke about reconciliation, and sat down again. The whole room was silenced, and the bishop said that there we had all the wisdom we needed.

Wisdom for a difficult life situation

Janice's husband left her for another woman. A new Christian, Janice was anxious to respond in a godly way, and waited patiently with an open heart. Her patience was rewarded, and her husband came back to her. But then he left again. Once more he returned; and again he left. Unsure how to handle the situation, Janice asked some of the leaders of the church to pray with her. As they prayed, Janice was released from a heavy weight which seemed to pin her to the ground. Then came an unexpected suggestion: she should take off her wedding ring. Janice, mindful of her wedding vows but clear that her husband would not be able to choose between her and his new partner, accepted this as a word of wisdom. She took off her ring, and asked her husband to decide whether he was leaving or staying. He left. Janice settled down to bring up her daughters, and some years later met, and married, William, a strong Christian.

Wisdom in knowing what to say

Recently I was invited to a local school. The Christian Union had dwindled to a regular attendance of about four, and the plan was to launch a programme for the new academic year. About twenty students crowded together in a small room, some Christian, some not. My daughter Katy asked the Holy Spirit to be with us, and I spoke on 'The meaning of life - does Christianity work?'. I spent the next hour dealing with a forest of stretching questions on everything from evolution to suffering - thanking God for the way my replies seemed to come easily despite the complexity of the topics, and to land in people's hearts and minds. Afterwards the teacher wrote: 'It made such an impact on some of them that even later that evening whilst I resumed my boarding house duty I was aware of this. One girl just lay on the sofa in the common room for the whole evening with the 'birthday feeling' saying 'Mrs Bennett, now I know!.' Attendance a the CU is now growing, and some of the students have begun going to church.

A word of knowledge

'To another is given a word of knowledge according to the same Spirit', Paul continues. And this is all, in this section of his letter, that he says about what is commonly called the gift of knowledge. Not surprisingly, interpretations have varied. Roughly speaking, charismatics tend to understand it as the supernatural revelation of information concerning one person to another person, whereas evangelicals are more likely to identify it with inspired teaching. The difficulty with the first is that it's hard to see how knowledge is then to be distinguished from prophecy. The difficulty with the second is that it's hard to see how knowledge is then to be distinguished from teaching - and in any case 'a word' of knowledge would produce a rather short piece of teaching!

What is clear, however, is that 'knowledge', or *gnosis*, was an important and particular issue for the Corinthians. 10 of the 29 New Testament uses of the word come in this letter, and most of the remainder in Paul's other writings. Paul, the apostle to the Gentiles, ministered mostly to people with a pagan rather than Jewish background, and it was out of such communities that the various 'gnostic' corruptions of the Christian faith would grow. Related both to Eastern cults and to the Greek mystery religions, these had in common the belief that salvation was attained in some way through a secret knowledge of the mysteries of the universe.[45] As with wisdom, Paul is at pains throughout this letter to help the Corinthian believers develop a Christian, rather than pagan, understanding of knowledge. It would seem that they had claimed that 'all of us possess knowledge', and that this knowledge justified, for example, the attending of idol worship and the eating of sacrificed food.[46] Paul here emphasizes that all knowledge, like wisdom, is given by the Spirit and bears witness to Jesus; it is not in any sense secret, and it does not come from within ourselves. He will go on in the next chapter to remind them that in any case to have prophetic powers and to understand all mysteries and all knowledge is of no value if we do not have love.[47] Whatever we know, we should know it in love.

It is helpful to ask ourselves what kind of knowledge Jesus seemed to have which was available to him through the Spirit but not available to those who had not yet been filled with the Spirit. Well, he knows that the Samaritan woman he meets at a well has had 5 husbands. He knows who will betray him. He knows all that will happen to him. He knows where the fish are in the sea of Tiberius.[48] Similarly, Peter knows that Ananias has lied about the money received from the sale of his field, and Paul knows that the ship in which he is sailing to Rome will be lost but that all those on board will survive.[49] In addition he often knows what he is to do, receiving this information in visions, dreams and through hearing voices. This is not without precedent - words of knowledge had been given on occasion to the Old Testament prophets – Elisha, for example, was able to warn the Israelite army to avoid places where the Arameans planned to lay an ambush.[50] But now the Holy Spirit makes such insights available to the whole body of Christ.

How do we recognise a word of knowledge today? However we choose to define it, it's clear that our own experience as Spirit dependent Christians offers us some ways of thinking about this gift.

The Spirit often seems to reveal things to us as we pray for one another – words or images which relate to a person's past or present circumstances but which are unknown to the individual receiving them. 'You will live to see your grandchildren', Linda, a single parent with young childre n, thought she heard God informing her as she received the news that she had cancer. She did. 'It's something to do with children, I saw you being bullied in a playground, and I think I was being given Proverbs 12.1', said Ann, praying in the kitchen for a friend meeting with two others in the next room, 'but that must be wrong, because you were praying about issues in the church weren't you?'. They weren't, and Ann had seen and heard correctly. 'There's a left handed man coming this morning with an injury to his right arm', said a member of our healing prayer team, who as he prayed had seen an image of a man wearing a watch on his right wrist. This word was given out during the service, and a man named Rob nervously came for prayer and was healed of a longstanding repetitive strain injury.

A word of knowledge in Tanzania

Dorisia is an illiterate woman of advanced years, and she lives in a small village outside the town of Dongo in the Kiteto region of Tanzania. Dorisia is a member of a *Rooted in Jesus* discipleship group. When her leader prayed for the group to receive the Holy Spirit, the Spirit came upon Dorisia, who immediately spoke in tongues. The next Sunday she rose to her feet in church – not usual for elderly illiterate women - and said 'I have to say that there is a woman here with a problem in her abdomen. I want to pray for her'. A woman stood – she'd been suffering from continuous bleeding, 14, 21 days each month. Together they prayed for her and she was instantly healed. Dorisia continues to receive words of knowledge and to pray for people in her village.

A word of knowledge in England

'I want to speak to you from the book of Isaiah', God said to Alice as she and Robert moved to the church of which Robert had just been appointed vicar. Alice eagerly read it – only to find she could not make head or tail of it. 'Must have got that wrong,' she thought. But within a few months, things had begun to go very badly for Robert. A small minority in the church began to push for his resignation, spreading lies and false accusations, writing angry letters to the bishop and sowing discord amongst the congregation. As people prayed, God began to speak – from the book of Isaiah. Promises of new things, of restoration, of blessing, of rebuilding. Alice cautiously highlighted them in her Bible, and Isaiah began to turn pink. One day Robert was praying with a colleague, who sensed they were being directed to Isaiah 41.10-12 – 'fear not; you will look for your enemies and find they are gone'. Hoping this might be true, Robert returned to his office. On the way he met Peter. Peter had his Bible open; I have a word for you - Isaiah 41.10-12.' Robert asked God for one more confirmation. The next day, in his car, he turned on the radio. 'Fear not; you will look for your enemies and find they are gone' said the radio, from Isaiah 41.10-12. Within months every one of the contentious minority had, for different reasons, left the church. Alice watched in delight as the pink bits of Isaiah gradually began to turn into reality. It was a slow process; but by the time Robert and Alice themselves moved on years later the church had grown into a vibrant community with hundreds of adults, students, teenagers and children involved in cells, worship groups, Alpha courses, outreach events and other activities, with a church plant and many active missionary partnerships abroad. God had indeed spoken, in the nick of time - from the book of Isaiah.

So a word of knowledge is perhaps most easily understood today as the receiving of information hidden from the person who receives it but needed for the benefit of one or more others.

The gift of faith

Paul next refers to the faith which is given by the Spirit. The word faith occurs frequently in the New Testament, but here it seems to be used in a particular way, broadly summed up by John Chrysostom in the 4th century when he distinguished between the faith which is concerned with belief and the faith which is concerned with miracles. The faith Paul writes about here is not the 'saving faith' which he mentions in Ephesians 2.8 and which recurs throughout the gospels in the invitation to repent and believe in Jesus. Nor can it be quite the same as the faith Paul mentions as a fruit of the Spirit, using the same word *pistis* and referring to something which grows in us over time as we learn to trust God. Rather it seems to be a special, Spirit-given faith received in circumstances of particular challenge, summarised by Jesus as the kind of faith which moves mountains and referred to in the same way by Paul in the next chapter.[51] Exercised in a context of prayer, this faith is not a kind of currency to buy miracles with (as in 'having enough faith'), but rather the supernatural confidence which results from a Spirit-given understanding of the plans and purposes of God.

Examples of this kind of faith are found throughout the Bible. Elijah was given such faith in the desire of God to overcome the prophets of Baal that he not only challenged them to a power contest but soaked with water the altar he would ask God to set on fire. Daniel, thrown into the lions' den by King Darius, emerged unharmed 'because he had trusted in his God'.[52]

In the New Testament faith is often linked with healing. Jesus sees the faith of the men who let their paralysed friend down through the roof, and heals him; he praises the faith of the centurion who knows that Jesus has only to say the word and his servant will be cured; he tells the woman who touches his cloak that her faith has made her well.[53]

Peter sees Jesus walking across the sea of Galilee and is able through faith to walk towards him. Paul sees that a cripple in Lystra is responding with faith to the good news of Jesus, and prays for his healing.[54] Faith, it seems, is not about how passionately we believe or want something, but about trust – a trust born of the confidence which comes from a spiritual insight into the grace of God. The word 'confidence' just means 'with faith' – and it's perhaps as good a summary as any of this gift.

So the gift of faith makes it possible to pray confidently for a particular outcome, not because we want it (though we may!) but because we have received the assurance that God wants it. When my husband was in intensive care after a near fatal road accident, we prayed for his recovery in the shared conviction that this was what God was asking us to do. To the surprise and delight of his doctors, he made a complete recovery. When a member of our church gave up his job and set off for an uncertain future working with street children in Brazil, we supported him in the shared faith that this was God's plan. Faith is an essential gift in the locker of anyone called into ministry – whether we take an initiative with a non Christian friend, take part in a parish mission, lead a church weekend away or run a conference for church leaders in Africa, we cannot do it if we do not receive the certain faith that God goes with us and indeed before us.

And yet we have to be careful. When a Christian believer in our neighbourhood took out a mortgage on a house he acknowledged he could not afford and named it, in big letters, 'Faith House', we waited with embarrassment for the inevitable repossession. When a Christian woman in a place we had lived previously insisted that God would not grow a new kidney for her husband because he did not have 'enough faith', we watched in dismay as his faith carried him ever stronger through years of dialysis, and hers withered and died.

The gift of faith allows us to watch God at work, and to play our part in his purposes. We need, as James suggested, to pray for it.

> *And this is the confidence we have in approaching God that if we ask anything according to his will, he hears us.*   1 John 5.14-15

Faith

Faith gives substance to our hope and convinces us of realities we do not see. Need I say more? Time is too short for me to tell the stories of Gideon, Barak, Samson, and Jephthah, of David and Samuel and the prophets. Through faith they overthrew kingdoms, established justice, saw God's promises fulfilled. They shut the mouths of lions, quenched the fury of fire, escaped death by the sword. Their weakness was turned to strength, they grew powerful in war, they put foreign armies to rout. Women received back their dead raised to life. others were tortured to death, refusing release, to win resurrection to a better life. others, again, had to face jeers and flogging, even fetters and prison bars. They were stoned to death, they were sawn in two, they were put to the sword, they went about clothed in skins of sheep or goats, deprived, oppressed, ill-treated. The world was not worthy of them. They were refugees in deserts and on the mountains, hiding in caves and holes in the ground. All these won God's approval because of their faith.

Hebrews 11, Revised English Bible

Esther turns her back on the witchdoctor

"One day when I came back from the Church from studying the Word of God my son started to cry continuously; all the night he cried. Next day my husband and brother-in-law told me that I am better to take my son to witchdoctor because he want grandfather name. I refused completely to go with my son to witchdoctor because I trust Jesus. After two days when my husband make preparation to find a hen to go with it to witchdoctor I attended the lesson, and when the time of prayer started I told my group members about my problem. They prayed for my son, and from that time my son stopped to cry. I told my husband that my son stopped to cry because we prayed for him in the Church. From that time my husband give me more time to attend the lessons" - Esther Ngau, Kiteto, Tanzania

Gifts of healings

If for the Corinthians tongues was the most prized of the gifts of the Spirit, I suspect that for many today healing would top the list. The ministry of healing is a vast and complex topic, but a number of points stand out from this particular passage.[55]

Firstly, Paul refers not to a 'gift of healing' but to 'gifts of cures', in a double plural which suggests that the gift comes not once to a person but afresh when needed, and that there are many different kinds of healing. So there is no such thing as a Christian healer, only a person through whom God sometimes chooses to work in this way (it is noticeable that when Paul lists the God-given offices of ministry he speaks of prophets, teachers, evangelists – but not healers).

Secondly, the noun 'cures' (*iamaton*) occurs nowhere else in the New Testament. It's a medical term (Luke, a doctor, uses the related verb 'to cure'), and is to be distinguished from the more common New Testament cluster of words based on the verb *sozo* which we translate variously as wholeness, healing and salvation. So it would seem that Paul here is talking not about the eternal, big picture healing we experience from sin, evil and death when we turn to Christ, but about those forms of healing which God gives in the context of this life – the kinds of things for which we go to the doctor.

As with some of the other gifts there seems to be an overlap between the gifts of healings and miracles. A miracle, in English, is 'something to be wondered at', and instantaneous physical healing is certainly to be wondered at. In Greek a miracle is a 'display of power'; and we read in the gospels that power went out of Jesus when he healed people.[56] So the distinction is not clearcut. It is probably simplest to say that all supernatural healings are miracles, but that there are also miracles which do not involve healing.

If there is an overlap between healings and miracles, there is also an interdependence between the gifts of healings, faith and discernment. Faith and healing are often linked in the gospels (though it seems faith is not always needed in order for a person to be healed). It is clear too that Jesus deals with similar needs in different ways, discerning different causes. Sometimes physical or emotional healing is needed, but sometimes Jesus offers deliverance ministry in outwardly identical circumstances.[57] Deliverance of course also depends on the active involvement of the Holy Spirit, but healing and deliverance are usually distinguished from one another in the gospel stories.

There are instances of healing in the Old Testament – the stories of Hezekiah and Naaman are particularly memorable.[58] But it is in the New Testament that healing comes to the fore. From the beginning of his ministry Jesus stated that healing was to be a key part of his mission, and in sending out his disciples to proclaim the good news of the kingdom his first instruction to them was to heal the sick and deliver the oppressed. 'If you do not believe me, believe my works, so that you may know and understand,' he said on another occasion.[59] We may conclude that healing is intended primarily as a sign of the of the compassion and grace of God for the lost, and not as a right or, still worse, as a kind of in-house perk for Christians. Do we have the courage to pray for the healing of those who do not yet know Christ as well as for those who do?

There are many, many instances of healing in the gospels and Acts – 18 of the 24 chapters in Luke, for example, include healing miracles. And yet healing is not in any sense guaranteed – Paul and Timothy both struggled with ill health.[60] There are many modern examples of physical healing, ranging from anecdotal healings of minor ailments to medically attested instances of healing from cancer, AIDS and paralysis.[61] Involvement for many years in the healing ministry has convinced me that John Wimber was right when he said that when we do not pray for healing, no one is healed, but that when we do, some are healed and some are not healed – so it's better to pray, and trust the outcome, physical, emotional and spiritual, to the Holy Spirit. Over the years I have prayed in depth for more than 200 people, mostly for inner healing, and my experience is that they usually do receive it. Healing of any kind is a sign of what is to come.

Gifts of healings

Sue, who had suffered from years of ill health, was at home recovering from a hysterectomy. She writes:

Despair and frustration had distanced me from God, blocking any road to personal contact with Him through prayer. I had deposited my frustration on anyone unlucky enough to share my company in this wilderness, including my hospital surgeon who I felt must be in some way responsible for my current pitiful state of 'health', with a gaping, infected abdominal wound which seven weeks after the operation still showed no signs of healing.

I was staring vacantly through my bedroom window, when I picked up the tattered 'remains' of Angela Unwin's *Patterns not Padlocks*. Her wisdom had helped me through many low points as a young exhausted Mum. Could she offer me anything to help me now in these dramatically different circumstances? She could. Realising that Christ always comes to us at our point of need, I discovered that I could use this spiritual blockage to become a starting point for prayer. And so began a summer of renewal and healing. Reminded repeatedly of the need to 'return and rest in quietness and trust' (Isaiah 30.15), I found that true silence can give space in which to be emptied so that God's grace could work in me; and I was reminded that I don't have to earn God's love - He loves me anyway!

I found myself in a position of trust and faith which allowed me to ask for God's healing. One Sunday evening recently my friend Alison came to pray with me. Afterwards I truly felt that God would be with me in the days to come and would heal me, at least from the spiritual illness which I had felt a few weeks earlier.

The physical wound is nearly healed now ('Truly amazing' according to the district nurse, having seen the 7 inch gap close by 5 inches in just a few days after Alison's visit) and I sit looking into my garden. At last alive to God's beautiful creation, His love for me and His healing power, I can see the birds soar heavenwards in the autumn air - and I feel I can go there too.

Only among intellectuals and in a scientific age is it thought to be too hard for God to heal the sick – Gordon Fee

Miracles

The word 'miracle' comes from the Latin verb 'to wonder at', and it is used to translate a quite different phrase used by Paul. To another, he says, the Spirit gives 'energisings of powers', *energemata dunameon*. So if we witness a miracle we should expect to see not just something unexpected or remarkable, but something which contains energy, something indeed which reminds us of dynamite. Something which can be explained only by reference to the same Spirit who once brought the universe into being in an explosion of power. Our role would seem to be no more than to be a channel of that power whenever God chooses to use it to intervene in the normal processes of nature.

Some commentators distinguish between miracles and healings by saying miracles are instantaneous whereas healings are gradual - but as there is only one recorded instance of Jesus performing a healing gradually (Mark 8, the blind man who first saw trees walking, and was able to identify the trees as men only after Jesus prayed a second time), and as the word 'power' is used repeatedly for healing, it seems to make more sense to distinguish between healing miracles and other miracles.

The Old Testament is full of miracles – the plagues sent upon the Egyptians, the parting of the Red Sea, the manna and quails provided each day in the desert, and the miracles performed through Elijah and Elisha. Jesus too performed many miracles – he turned water into wine, fed 5000 people with the lunch of a single boy, calmed a storm and restored at least three people to life: the son of a distraught widow, his friend Lazarus, and the little daughter of a synagogue leader named Jairus. In all cases the miracles seem to come not out of a desire on God's part to demonstrate his power, but out of compassion for the needs of his people.[62]

> Prayer is the most powerful form of energy that we can generate –
> Alexis Carrel, Nobel prize winner in physiology

Light in Cairo

In January 2008 a representative from an organisation called Open Doors, which works with persecuted Christians all over the world, was speaking at the Baptist Mainstream Leaders' Conference at Swanwick. She shared a story she had heard from a Christian minister with whom Open Doors is linked in Cairo. He told how one day his assistant asked if he could use the church minibus to bring the daughter of a local Muslim to church, at his request, to be prayed for – she had suffered from deep depression for years. Permission was given; the daughter was prayed for and received instant healing. They drove her and her father back home and as he turned his key in the door the whole flat filled with light. Father and daughter sat down in astonishment, received the light, and gave their lives to Christ. Then the father, curious, began to open doors – the coat cupboard, the bathroom, other rooms. The same light shone everywhere; bright, intense, warm. He ran to fetch the neighbours; they all sat together in the light. The next Sunday two minibuses were needed to get the man, his family and neighbours to the church. They all gave their lives to Christ. The father said, do you know – whenever I open the Bible, the light comes back...

Small miracle in Narok prison, Kenya

"I am sorry my sister for calling off your coming to prison during your visit. It wasn't safe. There were riots all night over them being beaten up by the guards and there was a lot of turmoil and unrest. I want to share with you a testimony of what happened that day; you remember praying shortly with me over the phone? Ten minutes after that prayer there was calm and immediately we got a letter of transfer of the officer in-charge who was actually the cause of the problems in this station. The testimony is we now have an open door not only in this prison but also in all the prisons in Rift Valley. One of the stations is Naivasha, which is a maximum security centre. It is the largest in East and Central Africa. I want to challenge you to pray for these programmes."

Your faithful Servant,
Ole Sagana Merus,
Prison Chaplain and Rooted in Jesus leader, April 2009

Prayer, whatever form it takes, is the greatest power in the world.
Through prayer men are healed, saved and born anew. In prayer we
enter for a while into the ceaseless movement of God's creative activity.
George Bennett

Miracles were a defining part of the life of the early church. Peter raises a girl named Tabitha from the dead in precisely the same way he had seen Jesus pray for Jairus's daughter. Paul restores to life a keen young man named Eutychus who, unable to stay awake, fell out of a window to his death late one night while listening to the gospel. Miracles are said to have occurred through both Philip and Stephen. An earthquake releases Paul and Silas from prison, Philip is transported miraculously from the Gaza road to Azotus, and Paul is bitten by a poisonous snake in Malta with no ill effect.[63]

Miracles are recorded throughout history and continue to take place today. A Nigerian pastor named Daniel Ekechukwu is said to have died in a road accident on Thursday November 30th 2001. He was taken to hospital, a death certificate was issued and his body dressed for burial. On the following Sunday, at the insistence of his wife, his body was taken to the basement of the Grace of God Mission church in Onitsha. As the service took place upstairs, Daniel's stiff body twitched and he began to breathe. Over the next few hours he gradually regained all his faculties. Nigeria is known for its love of hoax, but the most remarkable thing about this story, apart from the subsequent interviews with those involved including the medical staff who registered his death and dressed his body, is that Daniel's return to life was captured on video by someone who rushed down from the service upstairs with a camera.[64]

Miracles of healing are relatively easy to find, but not always involving buildings. In 2004 our church of Holy Trinity Leicester was found to have extensive dry rot in the foundations. We had called in an expert to investigate, but the further he went beneath the chancel and the organ the more dry rot he found. Led by a visiting Kenyan prayer leader called Utugi Kamau, who suggested that the physical condition of the church might be related to its spiritual condition, we found ourselves spending an evening in prayer and repentance for the pride and conflict which had recurred throughout the church's history. We sprinkled the floor with consecrated wine. The well known cold patch by the organ disappeared, the expert announced the following week that to his astonishment he could find no further trace of dry rot, and someone gave the money to fill in the hole and replaster the wall. A few weeks later we experienced a remarkable outpouring of the Holy Spirit during the service.[65]

Dealing with dry rot

When I put a leprous disease in a house, the owner of the house shall come and tell the priest. The priest shall examine the disease; if the disease is in the walls of the house, and if it appears to be deeper than the surface, the priest shall go outside to the door of the house and shut up the house seven days. The priest shall come again on the seventh day and make an inspection. If the disease has not spread in the house, the priest shall pronounce the house clean; the disease is healed. For the cleansing of the house he shall take two birds, with cedarwood and crimson yarn and hyssop, and shall slaughter one of the birds over fresh water in an earthen vessel, and shall take the cedarwood and the hyssop and the crimson yarn, along with the living bird, and dip them in the blood of the slaughtered bird and the fresh water, and sprinkle the house seven times. Thus he shall make atonement for the house, and it shall be clean.

To pray means to be willing to be naïve - Emilie Griffin

The deeper your desire to see God's answers, the deeper your hunger to see God at work, the more powerfully the Holy Spirit can pray through you. Holy desire is a holy power that energises prayer –
Wesley Duewel

An ordinary miracle

"Looking at those cars reminds me of what I can only call one of the many miracles we have experienced. In one of our visits to Northern Nigeria we were up in the north in Kaduna, and we had to get back to the capital Abuja that night. We had to get back for 2 reasons. First, because we were flying out on the cheapest kind of ticket. Some of you might know – bucket shop tickets. And in red all over them is stamped non refundable, non endorsable, non transferable, non everything - almost non usable ticket. And if you miss your plane, no other airline will pick up that bit of paper. Well, we had to get that plane – but also there was a debate in the Lords the next day on Africa. We wanted to bring the latest news from Nigeria. Our friends were running on Africa time. I'm not being critical, I run on it all the time. But it was 200 miles, Kaduna-Abuja. Pretty empty road, not much between the two, hundred miles done, hundred miles to go, clock watching, nail biting, very tight on time. A car coming the other way flags us down. We get out to see why; heart sinks. I'm no mechanic, but I know oil gushing out of rear wheel is not good news anywhere, least of all in the middle of the empty African bush, and not a soul in sight and a plane to catch. Desperate prayer. Two minutes later, out of empty bush, come two extremely competent young men, size up the situation, open up the boot, get out the tool kit, that wheel is off – fantastic. But nought for our comfort. As wheel comes off, wheel bearings all over the road. I'm no mechanic, but I do know you need wheel bearings to drive a car. Another desperate prayer. Two minutes later, out of that completely empty bush, comes a little lad, about 12 years old, with a black plastic bag. Out of black plastic bag comes brand new set of wheel bearings, that would fit a Honda car. In they go, on goes that wheel, fantastic. Well, that's fine, but the bright young lads say, just drive the car a few yards, and make sure that the other wheel's OK. Well it wasn't, wheel bearings coming out of that too. So they take it off, and wheel bearings all over the road, little lad comes back second time, second set of wheel bearings, fit a Honda car. You know, that car was on the road in 20 minutes. And I suggest to you that if your wheel bearings went in Shepton Mallet, there's no way you're going to get that car on the road in 20 minutes. But guardian angels come in wonderful forms, including little lads with black plastic bags with wheel bearings. Praise the Lord. We have a little motto in our organisation, we don't believe in miracles, we rely on them. Never take them for granted, but they happen when you need them."

Baroness Caroline Cox, speaking at New Wine, August 2007

Prophecy

The Greek word prophecy means 'speak for'. In the Old Testament a prophet had been a person anointed for life as the channel through whom God interpreted their situation to his people, and Paul recognises this kind of 'big picture' prophecy in his inclusion of prophets amongst the leadership offices of the church in Ephesians 4 and Romans 12. Here in 1 Corinthians 12, however, it seems he is talking about something slightly different.

The prophet Joel had said that one day God would pour out his Spirit on all people, and that not just appointed prophets but even young people and slaves, men and women, would prophesy. When the Spirit came on the disciples at Pentecost, Paul had recognised that this was now happening, and he says in 1 Corinthians 14 that every Christian should ask for the gift of prophecy so that they might encourage one another and build up the church.[66] It seems he has in mind therefore not a lifelong office, but that kind of prophecy which comes as a spontaneous word in the context of a gathering of believers, given not for the benefit of the speaker but for that of other persons present. Prophetic words of this kind have been called a 'miracle in the form of speech', and their purpose has been summarised as being for 'building up, stirring up, and cheering up' the Christian community.[67]

Just as the gift of prophecy is to be distinguished from the leadership office of a prophet, so it must be distinguished from that of a teacher. Most commentators stress the short, spontaneous nature of a prophetic word; it is a living word given for a specific moment and situation, and it carries within it the power to change the hearts and minds of those for whom it is intended.

Paul says that a prophetic word should always be weighed and tested. We are complex and fallible beings, and it is a great relief to know that God does not expect us to carry sole responsibility for the accuracy of any prophecy we may feel he is giving us. Nor does he necessarily make us responsible for the interpretation or the outcome of a prophetic word; God works through his own words to perform them, as he once reminded Jeremiah.[68] It is all too easy for us to ride our hobby horses, to speak out of frustration or be swayed by our own emotional issues. Truly prophetic words are usually surprising and seem somehow to carry an instantly recognisable authority which is independent of the speaker. Our role is to speak them, and leave them; like that of a postman, it comes to an end with delivery. When Agabus prophesied that Paul would be imprisoned in Jerusalem, there was a sharp disagreement about whether this meant he should go or not go. Agabus himself said nothing. Paul, to whom the prophecy was given, recognised it as a promise that the Lord would be with him, and went.[69]

The gospel with the most references to prophecy is John, himself a prophet. All the gospels include examples of prophetic speech – John the Baptist, Caiaphas, Zechariah, Simeon, Anna are all said to prophesy.[70] On one remarkable occasion a Syrian woman speaks prophetically to Jesus himself, suggesting he should minister not just to Jews but also to Gentiles.[71] In Acts Luke talks both about those who hold a prophetic office broader than any one community, such as Agabus, Judas and Silas, and also about people who speak prophetically on specific occasions, such as the daughters of Philip and the new believers in Ephesus.[72] Most prophetic words seem to be concerned with the present, but on occasion they may relate to the future. Many of Jesus's own prophecies have a future dimension – he announces the coming of the Spirit, warns the disciples that persecution awaits them, and tells Peter he will be taken where he does not wish to go.[73] Paul too sometimes speaks prophetically about the future, to Elymas, to the Ephesians, to his shipmates.[74]

Prophetic words continued to dominate the life of the early church. In the 3rd century Cyprian writes that many persons are called into the ministry of the church by means of a prophecy given by others; that visions and prophecies are received which offer comfort to those preparing for martyrdom; that prophecies give personal guidance and direction; and that the Lord speaks in this way in order to lead churches into unity at times of conflict.[75]

Today prophecy occupies a lower profile in the church, perhaps through our own dislike of disorder or fear of dominating personalities, but also to the detriment of our relationship with God. We have, as Jane Williams remarks, lost a great deal through fear of finding the Holy Spirit at work without our authorisation![76] But prophetic words play a key part in the guiding of individuals, in the building up of church fellowships, and in the birth and lives of organisations within the church.

When a Brazilian Christian prophesied that Sarah, then aged 18, was to be called to a big city in a country called Greece, Sarah (who, unknown to this woman, had been praying for Greece since the age of 13) was anxious. Following 1 Thessalonians 5.19-21 she began to test this prophecy. Over the next seven years it was confirmed through scripture and through the prayers and words of others, and eventually Sarah, by now a young fashion designer in Leicester, gave up her job and moved to Athens. Sarah now finds herself on the leadership team of Hellenic Ministries and involved in mission all over Greece. When a group of six elderly Methodists in Cornwall were offered £3.5 million for their chapel by a hotel developer, they prayed. 'God's got bigger ideas than that', one said. They turned down the offer, advertised for an outreach worker, and the chapel has now been transformed into a vibrant surf church packed with young people. [77]When a group of bishops praying together before the 1978 Lambeth Conference received a prophetic word to 'care for the nervous system of the body of Christ', they founded the international missionary organisation SOMA (Sharing of Ministries Abroad).

Thus the Lord cares for his church.

Let the prophet who has my word speak my word faithfully. Is not my word like fire, says the Lord, and like a hammer that breaks a rock in pieces? Jeremiah 23.28-29

Let two or three prophets speak, and let the others weigh what is said. 1 Corinthians 14.29

Do not despise the words of prophets, but test everything. 1 Thessalonians 5.20-21

A prophecy of blessing

In 2003 in a small and dusty town called Engusero, 99 evangelists had been meeting for two days to learn how to lead small groups using the *Rooted in Jesus* discipleship course which we developed at the request of our link diocese of Mount Kilimanjaro in Tanzania. The conference closed with a remarkable time of worship, marked by joy, fervour and the distribution of new spiritual gifts. As the Spirit moved among the people, silence fell, and one person stepped forward with a prophecy:

'I think God wants to say this to you. This is a beautiful place. But I know that life is hard here. In the eyes of the world, Kiteto is not an important place, and you are not important people. But I want you to know that in my eyes Kiteto is a very important place, and to me you are a special people. If you will seek me with all your heart, if you continue to praise and to pray as you have done today, then I will bless you.'

Four years later we returned to meet with those same evangelists. During the four years they had faithfully followed the leadership of their new bishop, John Hayden, and had taken their groups through the complete course. They were like different people; taller, more confident. They told us story after story of changed lives, of healings, of answers to prayer. This time we met not in a small brick church, but in a large, new cathedral in a compound containing a Christian college where people from the whole region could come to learn practical skills and deepen their understanding of God. In the same compound stood a new primary school and a complex of administrative buildings. Nearby was a hospital and a new borehole providing fresh water. In the villages there were new pastors' houses, church nursery schools, water filters and carts, and a scheme for group leaders to receive milk goats to help support their families. What advice did they have for new leaders in other places, we asked? 'Recognise that this is a call on your life,' they said; 'and depend on the Holy Spirit in everything you do. God keeps his promises.'

Discernment of spirits

The word Paul uses for the 'discernment' of spirits, *diakresis*, comes from the verb 'evaluate' or 'discriminate between'. The word for 'spirits' is the usual one, *pneumatikon*, which elsewhere in the New Testament is used in four ways: to refer to the spirit within the human person, to the Spirit of God, and to supernatural spirits which may be either angelic or demonic.[78]

We live in a physical universe, and over the centuries we have acquired a way of looking at the world which assumes that reality is primarily visible and material. We have become aware, thanks to Freud, Jung and their successors, that we also need to take into account emotional factors if we are to accurately interpret some situations; but we are less good at evaluating the spiritual dimension of reality. We can investigate the material world through scientific experiment, and we can understand a person through asking them questions about their experiences and listening to their feelings; but we have no natural way of gauging the spiritual dimension of a situation. And yet it is often the case that the key to a particular problem lies entirely here. This is why we need to seek the gift of discernment.

Paul says nothing more about discernment in this chapter, but he uses the same word again in chapter 14 when talking about the need to test prophecy. False prophets had long been a problem in Israel – we may recall the scorn with which God spoke to Ezekiel and Jeremiah of the false prophets of their day.[79] Paul himself, 'filled with the Holy Spirit', had recognised the Cypriot magician Elymas as a demonic prophet whose words were leading people away from Jesus; and he discerned that the prophecies given by a slave girl in Philippi were inspired not by the Holy Spirit but by a python spirit, and silenced her by casting it out. Jesus had done the same with a man in the synagogue at Capernaum.[80]

Discernment is needed not just in the case of prophecy, but also when praying for healing. Jesus knew when a person's affliction was purely physical in nature and when it had a spiritual cause – a woman with bleeding is healed by touch, but a woman with a bent back is healed when he casts a spirit out of her. A blind man is healed by anointing his eyes with mud, but a deaf man is healed by dismissing a spirit.[81] We can waste a lot of energy trying to deliver emotionally wounded people and counsel demonised people!

My husband prayed once with a young man who had recently married. Everything was going well – but Philip began to find that whenever he passed a young woman in the street his mind would be filled with unwelcome and inappropriate thoughts. Deeply ashamed, Philip had apologised to God and resolved to dismiss these thoughts. To his dismay, they kept on coming. In desperation he asked for prayer. Those praying discerned that his problem had a spiritual cause, and prayed for deliverance from evil. From that day Philip was no longer troubled in this way. Similarly, a missionary family working in Papua New Guinea found that the emotional and spiritual distress of their daughter went when the part of the house which contained her bedroom was cleansed of spiritual forces which had been there since warring tribes had fought over the land on which it was built.[82] There is sometimes more to our struggles than meets the eye.

We should also seek the gift of discernment when we are in certain places or situations. Utugi Kamau discerned that the real issue in Holy Trinity was not physical but spiritual. It is often the case when there is deep, apparently unresolvable conflict in a church that the real cause lies not in the human relationships where the conflict is being expressed, but amongst 'the spiritual forces of evil in the heavenly places,' as Paul writes to the Ephesians.[83] Such evil, and its cause, is revealed through discernment; it can be almost palpable.

Sometimes we need to discern when something comes not so much from a demonic spirit as from the human heart. 'That,' said Mike firmly when I told him something apparently plausible that had been said, 'is not of God.' Mike led our pre-service listening prayer sessions beautifully, always encouraging people to share what they felt they had received, always somehow knowing what was to be passed on to the congregation and what left in the privacy of the prayer room. The result was that people would respond to over 70% of the words given out, and many received healing as a result.

Jesus himself 'knew what was in everyone'. He welcomes Nathanael, saying as he sees him coming 'here is truly an Israelite in whom there is no deceit!', and renames Simon as Peter, the 'rock'.[84] The disciples in turn recognise him as more than a man, as the Son of God, and this too is a spiritual insight. Discernment enables us to see with the eyes of the Spirit, to know what is in the heart of a person.

Finally, we should seek discernment not just for the presence of demonic but also for that of angelic spirits, said by the writer to the Hebrews to be sent to serve us.[85] 'The angels are back', said Ann happily one Sunday morning some weeks after the resolution of a conflict in the church. I have learnt over the years in Africa that when we are asking the Holy Spirit to come, his arrival is usually heralded by that of a bird, often one which will fly in through the roof or windows and begin to sing from the rafters. I hear the bird; I know the Spirit.

Discernment of spirits

On holiday, we saw an advert for a medieval music group. We went to hear them. The group was German and their music was good; but the songs were explicit and they were adorned with skulls and various dark objects. As I stared in horrified fascination, our daughter, too small to understand the words or recognise the objects, went pale, began to tug at my hand, said she felt very sick and insisted 'we must go home NOW.' Within a few minutes of leaving, she was fine.

Worship in Kerugoya, Kenya, was unusually inharmonious. The team began to dread it, and to argue about what to do about it. We prayed for discernment and wisdom. The next morning we asked, who are we worshipping? 'Engai,' they said. 'God. He lives on Mount Kenya, and is the God of the Kikuyu tribe. The missionaries who first came told us his son is Jesus.' That afternoon we spent a lot of time in Deuteronomy 12 and John 4. The next morning a choirmaster led the worship – a melodious and newly composed song to the renewing power of God, Father, Son and Spirit. The atmosphere changed completely.

Some people seem to be more naturally gifted in discernment than others. From babyhood my daughter would wake crying whenever we were praying downstairs for a person whose difficulties turned out to be caused by demonic activity or influence – but never when we were praying for purely emotional or circumstantial issues. Others are particularly sensitive to disturbances in buildings; others are able easily to identify untruth or deception. We should seek this gift and learn to rely on those who receive it – to pray without discernment is a bit like doing car maintenance with your eyes shut!

Kinds of tongues and the interpretation of tongues

The gift of 'tongues' (or languages) is probably the most widely misunderstood and misappropriated of all the gifts of the Spirit. Paul insists (vs 30) that not all believers should expect to experience this, and it is clear from his long discussion in chapter 14 that the Corinthians, perhaps influenced by pagan practices, had prioritised this rather showy gift over all others – a mistake which has been made many times since then.

Tongues is the only gift not mentioned in the gospels, except by Mark, who relates a prophecy of Jesus that believers would speak in new tongues.[86] The classic example comes in Acts 2.4 when on the Day of Pentecost the disciples are filled with the Spirit and begin to speak in languages not known to themselves but understood by pilgrims from other nations. Tongues given in this way, Paul says, are for the benefit of unbelievers. But it seems that at other times the tongues spoken are not intelligible by natural means, and Paul distinguishes between human and angelic tongues. This second use of tongues seems to have been the experience in Corinth.[87]

Tongues spoken in this way in a gathering of believers are directed not to oneself or to others but to God; they are 'mysteries in the spirit', and are best regarded as vehicles of praise and prayer; they may be spoken or sung. Paul says that each person should pray for the interpretation of his own utterance, and that people should not all speak at once, so that each tongue may be interpreted if not by

Discernment of a spirit from West Africa

My parents had difficulty in conceiving. After 15 years, they went to a witchdoctor. His spells were efficacious and I was born. Aged 14, I was sent to my future mother-in-law's house. She, knowing my parents' difficulties, took me to a witchdoctor so that I would conceive. My husband went into politics. He was on the side of the government, and had quite a prominent position. He accompanied me to the hospital when I was pregnant with my second child. He was disgusted by the state of the hospital, and tried to get something done politically. When my third child was born, he found there had been no improvement. He joined the opposition. On New Year's Day 1997, we were arrested. He was effectively told to keep out of politics or be killed. He was very determined and wouldn't be silenced. In May 1997, he was murdered in police custody. I was helped to escape to England, with my youngest two children. My eldest, away from home at the time, was left behind.

For five years, Olive struggled to make a new life in Leicester, helped by Christian friends. She made much progress, but was locked into grief, self-pity and anger. One afternoon I met her with a discerning friend. When we began to pray, the main problem appeared to be her inability to forgive. She needed to forgive the President, the police, her husband ("if he hadn't been so obstinate this needn't have happened"), her mother-in-law, and her parents. We made little progress until, by the Holy Spirit, a word was revealed. I wrote the word, an African sounding word of about seven letters, on a piece of paper. It was the name of the controlling spirit of her parents' witchdoctor. Olive changed one letter from 't' to b'.

As soon as that happened, she was transformed. "That's it," she screamed, and behaved for a few minutes like a powerful witchdoctor — shouting, chanting, and displaying blazing eyes. After some quiet prayer the spirit was released. She slept for the next week, and soon afterwards was able to pray to forgive all those who had hurt her. We continued to pray for justice.

Occult problems may cling deeply to people, and make it hard for them to receive Christ and to forgive others. Olive had received Christ, but had been unable to make make any real spiritual progress. Two years after we prayed, her eldest son was brought to this country, remarkably, by one of her husband's political opponents. She celebrated with a party attended by many members of her church community.

Olive's story is told in ReSource magazine issue 7

the speaker then by someone else.[88] Proper interpretation is also important because it seems that not all tongues are inspired by the Holy Spirit. Tongues occur in other human cultures and may at times be demonic in origin (demonic tongues tend to sound harsh and unpleasant).[89] Speaking as a linguist, I find it curious that whereas many who speak in tongues are clearly caught into a different tonal range and pronunciation from their normal usage, others seem to speak their heavenly language with a pronounced English accent. It may be that some tongues come simply from the human mind.

The phenomenon of tongues has been curiously controversial. 'Do all speak in tongues?, Paul demands, with the clear implication that they do not. And yet many Christian churches teach that they should. 'Do not forbid speaking in tongues', Paul says clearly; and yet some denominations do just that.[90]

Should we ask for the gift of tongues? Paul says that it's scarcely the most important of gifts, and yet it does build us up. For years I did not seek it because I felt I'd be able to fake it. Then I found myself in Africa, often praying for people whose needs I could not ask about and whose languages I did not speak. At that point I asked for the gift, and received it through the prayer of a friend. It was an odd experience. As we prayed I remained reluctantly silent; until the Spirit told him to sing to me. He sang – so badly that I thought that if he was willing to do that, the least I could do was risk giving it a go. So I opened my mouth, and out came tongues – a gift which I have come to see as a kind of humbling of the mind before God. Since then I have used tongues regularly to pray for others, asking the Spirit to intercede for me as I do so. It seems from people's responses that he does.

If I speak in the tongues of mortals and of angels, but do not have love, I am a noisy gong or a clanging cymbal. 1 Corinthians 13.1

Tongues in Willesden

A secretary, quiet, unobtrusive, a member of Oak Tree Anglican Fellowship in north London – suddenly in church one day her voice was heard rising above the hymn. As the hymn ended, she continued to sing. Everyone listened in silence. Eventually she finished and sat down. An Iranian came forward, visiting the church with his wife, and said that she had been singing a beautiful song in High Persian to 'the prince of heaven'. 'Who is the prince of heaven?', he asked. Laughing, they explained. The Iranian committed his life to Christ. Afterwards he asked the secretary, 'Where did you learn my language?' He had been a university lecturer, and High Persian is used only amongst the highly educated. She of course had no knowledge of High Persian or anything like it; she was singing in the language of heaven.

Hildegard of Bingen receiving words from heaven in the 12th century

Tongues on the Tube

The captain of the HMS Glamorgan was returning from the Falklands War. On his way out to the South Atlantic he had been reading the Bible. On his return he was required to present himself at the Ministry of Defence, an appointment he kept in full uniform. Travelling through the Tube he was thinking over his faith and trying to decide about commitment. The train stopped between stations, and all the lights went out. In the sense of panic a large black man stood up, pointed down the carriage and said "Someone here has to give his life to the Lord Jesus!". The captain thought, "That's me!", and did. The lights came back on and the train moved on to the next station, where the captain got off. So did the large black man, through a door further down. The captain went up to him to thank him for what he had said. The man's companions explained that he didn't speak English.[84]

Other spiritual gifts

So Paul ends his discussion of spiritual gifts. He has rattled through them with very little explanation – but has devoted a great deal of attention to the image of Christian believers as different parts, differently gifted, of a single body; and above all to the overriding importance of love. Keep one thing, he says, and it wouldn't be the gifts, it would be the love. A warning to remember!

We saw earlier that it seems that Paul's major preoccupation is to facilitate the release of the Holy Spirit amongst believers, both for their own benefit and for that of non-believers. Our part is to open ourselves to the Spirit, and be ready to work in any way he chooses. These may be any of the ways Paul mentions in his letter to the Corinthians – or they may be others. Some of the other ways in which the Spirit works in or through us are listed below.

I have called by name Bezalel son of Uri son of Hur, of the tribe of Judah, and I have filled him with divine spirit, with ability, intelligence, and knowledge in every kind of craft, to devise artistic designs, to work in gold, silver, and bronze, tin cutting stones for setting, and in carving wood, in every kind of craft. Moreover, I have appointed with him Oholiab son of Ahisamach, of the tribe of Dan; and I have given skill to all the skilful, so that they may make all that I have commanded you.

Exodus 31.2-6.

The Mkonde woodcarvers in Tanzania. Most make traditional carvings – masks, figures, bowls. One told us that whenever he closes his eyes to imagine the carving he will make, only Christian images come into his mind. His open air workshop was filled with nativities, crucifixes, chalices and biblical figures – the only such workshop I have ever seen.

Spiritual gifts elsewhere in scripture

There is a man in your kingdom who is endowed with the spirit of the holy gods. In the days of your father he was found to have enlightenment, understanding, and wisdom like the wisdom of the gods. Your father, King Nebuchadnezzar, made him chief of the magicians, enchanters, Chaldeans, and diviners, because an excellent spirit, knowledge, and understanding to interpret dreams, explain riddles, and solve problems were found in this Daniel.

Daniel 5.11-12

You wrote 'it is well for a man not to touch a woman'... I wish that all were as I myself am. but each has a particular gift from God, one having one kind and another a different kind. To the unmarried and the widows I say that it is well for them to remain unmarried as I am. But if they are not practising self-control, they should marry.

1 Corinthians 7.1, 6-9

As in one body we have many members, and not all the members have the same function, so we, who are many, are one body in Christ, and individually we are members one of another. We have gifts (*charismata*) that differ according to the grace given to us: prophecy, in proportion to faith; ministry, in ministering; the teacher, in teaching; the exhorter, in exhortation; the giver, in generosity; the leader, in diligence; the compassionate, in cheerfulness.

Romans 12.4-8

But each of us was given grace according to the measure of Christ's gift (*doureas*). Therefore it is said, 'When he ascended on high he made captivity itself a captive; he gave gifts (*domata*) to his people'... The gifts he gave (literally, *he gave some to be...*) were that some would be apostles, some prophets, some evangelists, some pastors and teachers, to equip the saints for the work of ministry, for building up the body of Christ.

Ephesians 4.8-12

Above all, maintain constant love for one another, for love covers a multitude of sins. Be hospitable to one another without complaining. Like good stewards of the manifold grace of God, serve one another with whatever gift each of you has received. Whoever speaks must do so as one speaking the very words of God; whoever serves must do so with the strength that God supplies.

1 Peter 4.8-11

Getting started

My first experience of the work of the Holy Spirit as Paul describes it in his letter to the Corinthians came at a time of crisis. We were living in Corby, where Roger was the vicar of St Columba's. St Columba's was a friendly church, all yellow paint and green roof, brick built in the 50s in the middle of the new steel works housing estate. Solidly evangelical in its roots, it had grown through a steady flow of conversions, and by then consisted of about 120 townsfolk. The worship was noisy and joyful, and the midweek activities busy and varied. But things began to go wrong. The organist and the youth leader, both married, ran off together. The church began to be divided over this issue and others; the PCC became disrupted and contentious. The turning point came when a man named Trevor began to be drawn in. Rock solid in his faith and his family life, Trevor was a key person for the future growth of the church.

We didn't know what to do, except pray. So eight of us met together, shared a meal, then closed our eyes in confusion. And God began to speak. One person received a picture, another a passage of scripture. As we prayed, the images and the scriptures changed. A chain was broken. Peace came. The next Sunday Trevor was back to his old self. No one else was drawn in. So new and so powerful was the experience that we continued to meet together regularly. We called the group 'Eagles', from God's promise to Isaiah that those who wait for the Lord woud rise up with wings like eagles. Many things happened in that group: the healing of broken hearts, the power to live in dysfunctional families, the removal of spiritual opposition to growth, and deep personal renewal and encouragement - and all we had done was wait on God in silence and desperation. No one had laid hands on us; none of us had experienced anything dramatic. The Spirit had taught us himself.

When we moved to Leicester, we found a church far ahead of us in its experience of spiritual gifts. There was a healing prayer team led by Mike and Ann. Before every communion service the team would meet in an upper room and wait on God in silence. Mike would encourage people to share what they had received – scriptures, impressions, convictions, images. As each made their contribution, Mike would ask others whether they could confirm it, until together the group built up an understanding of the prayer situations they would meet in the service. Mike would withdraw and pray over the various contributions, asking the Holy Spirit to confirm and order them for him; he would then offer what he felt was from God to the congregation.[92] Sometimes the team would imagine things, or speak from their own issues; but under Mike's gentle leadership gradually people learned to distinguish between what was from God and what was not. And week by week people would come for prayer, many of them to experience healing.

As time went on we decided to develop the prayer we offered and to form what we called a prayer ministry team. Drawn from the more experienced members of the healing team, this team consisted of people who would pray in pairs over a period of two or three hours for individuals whose needs could not be adequately addressed in the context of a Sunday service. I have now prayed, always with a partner, for over two hundred people in this way. We spend an hour or so listening, getting our minds round the issues, helping the person to clarify what it is they wish to bring to God in prayer. And then we pray – sitting, eyes closed, in silence, and waiting. The same thing happens: images, scriptures, words of knowledge. We ask for wisdom and discernment. We pray for healing. I used to dread each session, knowing I lacked the skills to bring peace to people's troubled lives, doing it only because I believed, through a dream, that this was what God required of me. I've learnt that although the listening part takes concentration, compassion, and the ability to understand another person, the praying part is not much more complicated than climbing into the passenger seat of a car. The Holy Spirit works as he will; we just have to be willing to be open to him.[93]

There are many ways of getting started and many ways of using the gifts of the Spirit. It is not difficult. It requires no special abilities except the willingness to be open, together, to the purposes of God. The Holy Spirit teaches us to pray as we ought. We really have to do little more than shut up, sit down in humility, ask him to meet with us and, last but not least, be willing to risk embarrassment.

Suggestions for ways forward:

In a small group

One place to start is in a small group. You may be part of a cell or home group, or a prayer group. Talk to the group about the spiritual gifts; suggest that each member read this book. When they have done so, do the group study which follows together. You may wish to follow this up by setting aside an evening to wait on God. Agree that you will not, on this occasion, offer any intercessory prayer, but that you will simply listen to God. You may wish to divide into threes and pray in silence for one another, asking the Spirit to meet with you as you do so. You may wish to focus on a particular issue in the life of your church or community – again, by listening rather than interceding. Spend as long in silence as you are comfortable with and then encourage people to share anything they feel they have received during the prayer time.

In a prayer triplet

You may belong to a prayer triplet. Share your personal concerns with one another and then spend time waiting on God in silence, each praying for the other two members. Then share any thoughts or scriptures which come to mind, and then pray again for discernment and confirmation. Someone has to be brave enough to go first – but it often happens that God speaks to different people in the same way at the same time, and this helps us know that we are hearing correctly. Always begin by inviting the Holy Spirit to be with you.

By yourself

Remind yourself that the gifts of the Spirit are the tools of our trade, the working tools we need in order to play our part in the continued mission and ministry of Jesus. Choose an ordinary day, and begin by reading John chapter 4, where Jesus meets the woman at the well. Try consciously listening to the Spirit as you go about your daily business. Respond to him in every way you can. See what happens! You may like to do this with a friend, and compare notes afterwards. If you find that the Spirit works in and through you, do it again. Can you make it a lifestyle?

Read some of the books listed at the end of this book.

<u>As part of your church fellowship</u>

Find out what courses and materials are available to help you grow in your dependence on the Holy Spirit. Possiblities include:

- The Lent course *Season of Renewal* by Alison Morgan and Bill Goodman offers a gentle way into greater dependence on the Holy Spirit. Consider whether you might use it with a group in your church.

- The ReSource healing course *In His Name* provides a practical introduction to the healing ministry, and includes a session on the gifts of the Spirit.

- For an excellent short article on how to start a healing group in your local church see Mike Hutchinson's contribution to ReSource magazine issue 1 'Healing and Evangelism'– or read it online: www.resource-arm.net/articles/healing_group.html.

Doing what Jesus did – a fresh look at the gifts of the Spirit

A group Bible study

"The Spirit of the Lord is upon me, because he has anointed me to bring good news to the poor. He has sent me to proclaim release to the captives and recovery of sight to the blind, to let the oppressed go free, to proclaim the year of the Lord's favour."   Luke 4.18-19

How can we escape if we neglect so great a salvation? It was declared at first through the Lord and it was attested to us by those who heard him, while God added his testimony by signs and wonders and various miracles, and by gifts of the Holy Spirit, distributed according to his will.
                                                          Hebrews 2.3-4

The Holy Spirit equips us to play our part in the continued mission and ministry of Jesus. 1 Corinthians 12 offers a description of some of the resources he offers to us as we seek to be faithful to that calling.

What follows is a group study to help people gain a deeper understanding of the Holy Spirit and his gifts. People will benefit more from the study if they read *Doing what Jesus did* before you meet together.

Timing
- Introduction and welcome – 10 minutes
- 1 Corinthians 12 reading and group work – 20 minutes
- Discussion of the gifts – 60 minutes
- Prayer – 30 minutes

Introduction and welcome   10 minutes

Open by reading Luke 4.18-19 to the group. Remind them that Jesus gave us the task of continuing this ministry, and promised that he would send the Holy Spirit to us to help us do this. Spend a few moments in prayer. You may like to sing a song of worship together as you open yourselves to God.

Ask someone to read Hebrews 2.3-4. Point out that we 'cannot escape' what Jesus has done for us, and we cannot live as if he had not done it. That means we need to open ourselves to the Spirit and his gifts, which God distributes among us according to his will.

Explain that the purpose of the meeting is to try and take a fresh look together at the gifts of the Spirit. So often we just rattle them off, making assumptions about what Paul means by each phrase he uses, without taking the time to consider them in the light of the ministry of Jesus or place them in the context of other relevant passages of scripture. Paul is clear that the gifts are given to the church as a whole, and not to us as individuals, so it makes sense to think about them together rather than in independent isolation.

1 Corinthians 12.1-11 reading and small group work

20 minutes

Read aloud the following passage, drawing attention to the literal meaning of the words (given in brackets).

[1]Now concerning spiritual gifts (spiritual things - *pneumatika)*, brothers and sisters, I do not want you to be uninformed. [4] Now there are varieties of gifts (graces – *charismata*), but the same Spirit; [5] and there are varieties of services (ministries or service – *diakonion*), but the same Lord; [6] and there are varieties of activities (energisings – *energematon*), but it is the same God who activates all of them in everyone. [7] To each is given the manifestation of the Spirit (manifestations – *phanerosis*) for the common good. [8] To one is given through the Spirit the utterance of wisdom (a word of wisdom), and to another the utterance of knowledge (a word of knowledge) according to the same Spirit, [9] to another faith by the same Spirit, to another gifts of healing (gifts of cures) by the one Spirit, [10] to another the working of miracles (energisings of power), to another prophecy, to another the discernment of spirits (discriminating between spirits), to another various kinds of tongues (languages), to another the

interpretation of tongues. [11] All these are activated by one and the same Spirit, who allots to each one individually just as the Spirit chooses.

Put people into twos or threes and give them each a specific gift to consider (you may like to put tongues and interpretation of tongues together). Ask them to spend 20 minutes looking up some of the references below. Tell them that you will then ask them to share with the group what new insight they have been given into the gift they are considering, and what most excites them about it.
After 15 minutes bring them back together.

Notes for small group work

1. A word of wisdom

Note: background – pagan understanding –mystery religions and esoteric pagan philosophies

- 1 Cor 1.17-2.16 wisdom is 'knowing the mind of Christ'
- Wisdom literature - Proverbs 1.20-33; 4.5-6; 8.22-31
- Joshua – Deut 34.9; Joseph – Gen 41.38-39; Solomon – 1 Kings 3.16-28
- Luke 4.32, Matthew 13.54 – all are astonished at his wisdom
- Jesus - answers difficult questions with wisdom - Mark 2.23-28 (sabbath); 3.22-27 (deliverance); 7.5-16 (washing)
- Jesus – his answers are theological, ie they derive from the nature of the kingdom of God, and not from law/custom

2. A word of knowledge

Note: background – pagan understanding – gnosticism – secret knowledge of the mysteries of the universe

- 1 Cor 8.1-2; 13.2
- Jesus – what knowledge did he have which was available to him through the Spirit alone? – John 4.16-18 (five husbands); 13.11 (who will betray him); 18.4 (what will happen to him); 21.4-6 (fish)
- Paul – Acts 5.3 (Ananias); 27.21-26 (shipwreck)
- Elisha forewarns against ambush (2 Kings 6.8-10)

3. Faith

Note: John Chrystostom distinguished between the faith which is concerned with belief (saving faith) and the faith which is concerned with miracles (mountain moving faith).

- Mark 11.22-24, 1 Cor 13.2 – the kind of faith which moves mountains
- Elijah & the prophets of Baal, 1 Kings 18.17-40
- Daniel and the lions, Daniel 6.23
- Jesus – Luke 5.20, faith of those who brought the paralysed man; 7.9, faith of centurion; 8.48, faith of woman who touches his cloak
- Peter – Matt 14.28, Peter walks on water
- Paul – Acts 15.8-9, cripple in Lystra has the faith to be healed

4. Gifts of cures

Note: *Iamaton* – medical term, 'cures', used nowhere else in the New Testament. Luke uses the related verb. To be distinguished from *sozo* – wholeness, healing, salvation. 'Gifts of cures' – the kinds of things for which we go to the doctor.

- Hezekiah - 2 Kings 20.1-11
- Naaman - 2 Kings 5.1-4
- Luke – 18 out of 24 chapters include healing miracles
- Ill health remains – Paul (Galatians 4.13), Timothy (1 Timothy 5.23)
- John Wimber – when we do not pray for healing, no one is healed. When we do, some are healed and some are not. It's better to pray.

5. Energisings of power

Note: *Energamata dunameon* – energisings of power. Jesus' miracles always come out of compassion for the pain of people.

- Plagues sent on the Egyptians (Exodus 7); parting of Red Sea (Exodus 14); manna and quails (Exodus 16)
- Elijah (1 Kings 17-18) and Elisha (2 Kings 2-4)
- Jesus – water into wine (John 2); feeding of 5000 (Matt 14); calming of storm (Luke 8); raising of widow's son (Luke 7); of Lazarus (John 11); of Jairus's daughter (Luke 8)
- Peter – raising of Tabitha (Acts 9)
- Paul – restoration of Eutychus (Acts 20)
- Philip and Stephen (Acts 6, 8)

6. Prophecy

Note: Means 'speak for' in Greek. 'A miracle in speech.'

- Joel 2.28-30
- Big picture prophets – Isaiah, Ezekiel, Jeremiah et al; Ephesians 4, Romans 12
- 1 Peter 2.20, 1 Thessalonians 5.20-21 – prophecy and its interpretation
- 1 Cor 14.3 – prophecy is for all, for 'building up, stirring up, cheering up' believers
- Prophecy in New Testament – the daughters of Philip, the Ephesians (Acts 19, 21)
- Jesus – coming of Spirit (John 14.26); warning of persecution (15.15-20); Peter's future (21.18).
- Paul – blindness of Elymas (Acts 13), his own future to the Ephesians (Acts 20); shipwreck (Acts 27)

7. Discriminating between spirits

Note: 'Spirits' (pneumatikon) in scripture usually refers to any of the human spirit / spirit of God / supernatural spirits either demonic or angelic.

- Ezekiel ch 13, Jeremiah 23 – false prophets
- Jesus – demonised man in Capernaum (Mark 1.21-27); woman with bent back (Luke 13.11), deaf man (Luke 11.14)
- Paul and Elymas (Acts 13.6-12), slave girl (16.16-18)
- Jesus – knowing what is in the heart of Nathaniel (John 1.47) and Peter (Matt 16.18)

8. Kinds of tongues (languages) and interpretation of tongues

Note: Paul seems to indicate two types of tongues, commonly referred to as xenolalia (foreign tongues) and glossolalia (angelic tongues).

- Mark 16.17 (NB some think this 'longer ending' of Mark was added later)
- Acts 2.3 (Pentecost); 10.46 (new believers in Caesarea); 19.6 (and in Ephesus)
- 1 Cor 13.1 – human or angelic tongues
- 1 Cor 12.30 – do all speak in tongues?
- 1 Cor 14.39 – do not forbid tongues

Discussion of the gifts   60 minutes

Invite a member of each small group to share what most struck or
excited them about the gift they considered, and allow the group to
respond. Allow 7-8 minutes for each gift.

Prayer   30 minutes

Spend 30 minutes in prayer. How you do this will depend on the
experience of the group.

- You may like to begin by inviting the Holy Spirit to be present, spend
  some time listening, and then share any words, pictures or
  impressions people may have received. If there is a current issue of
  direction or concern in the church or community you may wish to
  encourage people to focus on this issue.

- You may prefer to put people into threes and ask them to pray for
  one another that the Holy Spirit would equip them with the gifts
  they need when they need them; or to share something about
  themselves – a need, a desire, a prayer – and then spend some time
  praying for one another in turn.

Part 3 : The ministry of Jesus

Gifts of the Spirit in John, Luke and Acts

The ministry of Jesus and his disciples was characterised by the empowering presence of the Holy Spirit, and all the gifts mentioned by Paul in his letter to the Corinthians are clearly recognisable in the gospels and in the Acts of the Apostles – though not always as neatly as Paul's listing might suggest. The following study is not intended to be definitive; I offer it as an at-a-glance listing of examples, the main purpose of which is to demonstrate the links between 1 Corinthians 12 and the ministry of Jesus and the early church.

Wisdom
Knowing how to live or behave in a specific context in accordance with God's plans and purposes

John
Interpreting events and teaching from scripture:

John 1 – 'In the beginning was the Word...' – John reinterprets Genesis in the light of the coming of Jesus

John 7.14-16 – Jesus teaches in the temple at the festival of Booths. The Jews are astonished, and say, 'how does this man have such learning, when he has never been taught?' Jesus answers, 'my teaching is not mine but his who sent me'.

John 13.18 – 'it is to fulfil the scripture, the one who ate my bread has lifted his heel against me'.

John 15 – teaching about the true vine

Luke
Interpreting events and teaching from scripture:

Luke 2.40, 47 – the boy Jesus grew and became strong, filled with wisdom. Teaching in the temple at age 12, 'all who heard him were amazed at his understanding and his answers'.

Luke 4.14-15 – 'filled with the power of the Spirit, Jesus began to teach in synagogues and was praised by everyone.'

Luke 4.18-24 – Jesus announces that Isaiah 61 has been fulfilled

Luke 4.32 – in Capernaum 'they were astounded at his teaching, because he spoke with authority'.

Luke 7.22 – Jesus sends word to John the Baptist saying Isaiah 61 is fulfilled.

Luke 19.46 – driving sellers from temple quoting Isaiah 56.7; 'it is written, my house shall be a house of prayer, but you have made it a den of robbers'.

Luke 22.36-37 – Jesus says that what is written about him (Isaiah 53.12) is being fulfilled, and warns they now need swords

Luke 24.27 – 'beginning with Moses and all the prophets he interpreted to them (Cleopas & his companion) the things about himself in all the scriptures.

Luke 24.44 – 'these are my words that I spoke to you.. that everything written about me in the law of Moses, the prophets, and the psalms must be fulfilled. Then he opened their minds to understand the scriptures.'

Wisdom in knowing what to say:

Luke 5.36 et passim – teaching in parables

Luke 6 – sermon on mount and parables, et passim

Luke 9.49 – Jesus answers a question about someone exorcising in Jesus' name who 'does not follow with us'.

Luke 12.12 – When brought before synagogues, rulers, and authorities, 'the Holy Spirit will teach you at that very hour what you ought to say'.

Luke 20.23 – when his authority is questioned, Jesus responds with a question of his own – 'whose head and whose title does (this denarius) bear?'

Luke 21.14-15 – when brought before kings and governors, 'make up your minds not to prepare your defence in advance; for I will give you words and a wisdom that none of your opponents will be able to withstand or contradict'.

Making decisions:

Luke 6.12-13 – Jesus spends the night in prayer and chooses the disciples

Acts

Interpreting events and teaching from scripture:

Acts 1.16 – Peter shows how scripture foretold Judas (Ps 69.25, 109.8).

Acts 2.16-36 – Peter teaches from scripture on the coming of the Holy Spirit at Pentecost (Joel); and on the resurrection (Ps 16 and 110).

Acts 3.22 – Paul quotes Moses on the prophet who is to come (Deut 22).

Acts 4.11 – Peter teaches on Jesus as the cornerstone (Ps 118.22, Is 28.16).

Acts 4.24-28 – the gathered believers recognise Jesus as Messiah (Ps 2.1).

Acts 6.10 – Stephen speaks with great wisdom by the Spirit.

Acts 7 – Stephen speaks of God's dealings with Hebrew people from Abraham onwards.

Acts 8.30-35 – Philip explains the gospel to the Ethiopian eunuch (Is 53).

Acts 13.16-41 – Paul expounds the gospel from scripture, beginning with the exodus (Ps 2, Is 49).

Acts 17.2-3 – Paul expounds the gospel from the scriptures in Athens.

Acts 28 – Paul expounds the gospel from the Law and the Prophets, and quotes Isaiah's warning that it would not be accepted by the Jews, but embraced by the Gentiles.

Wisdom in knowing what to say or how to solve problems

Acts 6.1-6 – the disciples choose 7 men to serve at tables who are full of the Spirit and wisdom.

Acts 15.13-21 – James quotes Jeremiah, Amos and Isaiah and suggests the Gentiles should not be subject to circumcision.

Acts 17.23 – Paul preaches to the Athenians from their altar to an unknown God.

Acts 23.6 – Paul says he is on trial because of his belief in the resurrection – thus dividing Pharisees from Sadducees on the Council.

Acts 24-26 – Paul defends himself before Felix, Festus and Agrippa.

Knowledge
Receiving information supernaturally

John

John 1.42 – Jesus is introduced to Simon Peter, looks at him and says 'you are Simon son of John. You are to be called Cephas'.

John 4.16-18 – Jesus tells the Samaritan woman she has had 5 husbands

John 6.15 – Jesus realises they are about to make him king by force, and withdraws

John 13.3 – 'Jesus, knowing that the Father had given all things into his hands, and that he had come from God and was going to God, got up from the table, took off his outer robe..' and washed the disciples' feet.

John 13.11; 25-26 – 'he knew who was to betray him', and gives him bread

John 18.4 – 'Jesus, knowing all that was to happen to him...'

John 21.6 – Jesus appears to the disciples by the sea of Tiberius, and tells them where to catch fish.

Luke

Luke 2.26-27 – 'It had been revealed to (Simeon) that he would not see death before he had seen the Lord's Messiah.' Guided by the Spirit.. he recognises the baby Jesus.

Luke 5.4-6 – Jesus tells Simon where the fish are

Luke 19.30 – Jesus knows where there is an unbroken colt tied.

Luke 22.10-12 – Jesus tells Peter and John to meet a man carrying a jar of water, follow him into a house, and speak to the owner. He will show them a large room upstairs where they can prepare the Passover meal.

Acts

Acts 5.3 – Paul knows that Ananias and Sapphira have lied about the amount raised from the sale of their field.

Acts 20.22-23 – Paul tells believers in Miletus he is captive to the Spirit, and learns from him in every city that imprisonment and beatings await him.

Acts 26.12-18 – Paul tells Agrippa what Jesus said to him on the Damascus Road.

Acts 27 – Paul knows the ship will be subject to storms if it sails; he sees an angel in the ensuing storm, and knows the whole crew will be saved and that they should run the ship aground.

Faith
The confidence which comes from a spiritual insight into the grace of God

John

John 2.5 – at the wedding in Cana, Mary tells Jesus the wine has run out, and says to the servants, 'do whatever he tells you'. This was 'the first of his signs', revealing his glory; 'and his disciples believed in him'.

John 4.42 – the people of the Samaritan village believe because of the woman's testimony and because of what they hear for themselves; 'we know that this is truly the Saviour of the world'.

John 4.50 – Jesus tells the official in Capernaum that his dying son will live. 'The man believed the word that Jesus spoke to him and started on his way'. The boy is healed, and the man and his household believe. A gift of faith at a specific moment leads to a lifetime of faith.

John 9.6-7 – Jesus puts mud/saliva on the blind man's eyes at the pool of Siloam and he is healed. The man responds by believing; the Pharisees do not. Some say, surely we are not blind, are we?

John 10.22-27 – the Jews ask to be told plainly if Jesus is the Messiah. He says he has . told them, but they do not believe because they do not belong to him. They have not been given a gift of faith.

John 12.37-40 – Although he had performed so many signs in their presence, they did not believe in him. This was to fulfil the word spoken by the prophet Isaiah.. he has blinded their eyes and hardened their heart.' They have received no gift of faith.

Luke

Luke 5.12 – a leper tells Jesus that if he chooses, he can make him clean. Jesus heals him.

Luke 5.20 – on seeing the faith of the friends of the paralysed man, Jesus heals him.

Luke 7.9 – Jesus is astonished at the faith of the centurion in his power to heal; 'only speak the word, and let my servant be healed'.

Luke 7.50 – Jesus tells the woman who anoints his feet that her faith has saved her.

Luke 8.48 – Jesus tells the woman with the haemorrhage that her faith has made her well.

Luke 17.19 – Jesus heals 10 lepers and tells the one who returns to thank him that his faith made him well.

Luke 18.42 – Jesus heals a blind beggar outside Jericho, and tells him his faith has saved him.

Acts

Acts 3.16 – Paul says of the crippled man: 'by faith in his name, his name has made this man strong; and the faith that is through Jesus has given him this perfect health in the presence of all of you'.

Acts 11.24 – Barnabas was a good man, full of the Holy Spirit and of faith.

Acts 14.9 – in Lystra Paul sees that a man who had never had the use of his feet has the faith to be made well.

Healings
The cure of physical, emotional and spiritual disease

John

John 4.50 – healing of son of official in Capernaum.

John 5.8-13 – Jesus heals the man at the pool of Bethesda. The man says he doesn't know who Jesus is; he has been healed without faith.

John 6.2 – a large crowd follows him 'because they saw the signs he was doing for the sick'.

John 9.6-7 – Jesus puts mud/saliva on the blind man's eyes at the pool of Siloam and he is healed.

Luke

Luke 4.35 – Jesus delivers a man with unclean spirit, who is thrown down but gets up healed.

Luke 5.13 – Jesus touches a leper who is made clean.

Luke 5.20-25 – Jesus heals the paralysed man both of his sins and of his paralysis.

Luke 6.18-19 – Jesus heals the sick and cures those troubled with unclean spirits; 'power came out from him and healed all of them'.

Luke 7.2-10 – Jesus heals the centurion's slave at a distance.

Luke 7.21 – 'Jesus had just then cured many of diseases, plagues and evil spirits, and had given sight to many who are blind.'

Luke 8.2-3 – Jesus has cast 7 demons out of Mary Magdalene; Joanna, Susanna and others who now provide for him have been 'cured of evil spirits and infirmities'.

Luke 8.29 – Jesus casts the unclean spirits out of the Gerasene demoniac and allows them to enter a herd of swine.

Luke 8.44 – the woman suffering from haemorrhages is healed on touching Jesus' clothes.

Luke 9.1-2 – the 12 are sent out with power and authority over all demons and to cure diseases, to proclaim the kingdom of God and to heal.

Luke 9.11 – In Bethsaida, Jesus 'healed those who needed to be cured'.

Luke 9.42 – Jesus delivers a boy with an unclean spirit who convulses, foams and shrieks; 'Jesus rebuked the unclean spirit, (and) healed the boy'.

Luke 10.8-9 – Jesus sends out the 70 to 'cure the sick who are there, and say to them, "the kingdom of God has come n to you".'

Luke 11.14 – Jesus casts out a demon that was mute, and the person speaks.

Luke 13.11-13 – Jesus casts out a spirit from a woman who has been crippled and unable to stand straight for 18 years.

Luke 14.2-4 – Jesus heals a man with dropsy.

Luke 17.14 – Jesus heals 10 lepers by telling them to go and show themselves to the priest; they are healed as they leave.

Luke 22.51 – Jesus heals the ear of the high priest's slave after Peter has cut it off.

Acts

Acts 3.2-10 – healing of the crippled beggar at the temple gate in Jerusalem.

Acts 5.15-16 – the sick are healed by Peter's shadow falling on them, and all those brought from nearby towns are cured.

Acts 8.7 – in Samaria the paralysed and lame are cured and people delivered as Philip preaches.

Acts 9.33-34 – a bedridden man, Aeneas, is healed in Lydda through Peter.

Acts 10.38 – Peter tells how Jesus was anointed by the Holy Spirit and healed all those oppressed by the devil.

Acts 14.8-10 – a man who has never walked is healed in Lystra through Paul.

Acts 14.19-20 – when the disciples surround him, Paul, left for dead after being stoned gets up and goes back into Lystra.

Acts 28.8 – the father of Publius is healed from fever and dysentery when Paul lays hands on him.

Acts 28.9 – all the sick in Malta come and are cured.

Miracles
Acts of extraordinary supernatural power

John

John 1.1-3, 14 – the Word creates life and becomes incarnate.

John 2.7-11 – Jesus turns water into wine, 'the first of his signs', revealing his glory; 'and his disciples believed in him'.

John 2.23 – many in Jerusalem 'believed in his name because they saw the signs that he was doing'.

John 5.21 – 'just as the Father raises the dead and gives them life, so also the Son gives life to whomever he wishes'.

John 6.11 – Jesus feeds a large crowd with 5 loaves and 2 fish, leaving 12 baskets of leftovers.

John 6.19 – Jesus walks 'about 3 or 4 miles' over the sea of Galilee in a storm.

John 10.39 – 'they tried to arrest him again, but he escaped from their hands'.

John 11.41-44 – Jesus restores Lazarus to life from the tomb.

John 18.6 – 'When Jesus said to them, "I am he," they stepped back and fell to the ground.'

John 20.19 – Jesus appears in a locked room where the disciples are.

John 20.26 – a week later, Jesus again appears in a room with closed doors.

John 20.30 – Jesus did many other signs in the presence of his disciples 'which are not written in this book'.

Luke

Luke 1.24 – Elizabeth, barren and getting on in years, conceives following a prophecy from an angel.

Luke 1.35 – Mary, a virgin, conceives when the Holy Spirit comes upon her.

Luke 4.29-30 – Jesus walks through angry members of the Nazareth synagogue who try to hurl him off a cliff.

Luke 7.14-15 – Jesus raises the son of the widow of Nain.

Luke 8.24 – Jesus calms a storm on the lake of Galilee.

Luke 8.54-55 – Jesus raises Jairus's daughter.

Luke 9.16-17 – Jesus feeds more than 5000 with 5 loaves and 2 fish.

Luke 9.28-36 – The Transfiguration - Jesus talks with Moses and Elijah.

Luke 9.54 – James and John offer to command fire to come down on an unwelcoming Samaritan village.

Luke 10.13-14 – The 'deeds of power' done in Chorazin and Bethsaida would have caused Tyre and Sidon to repent.

Luke 19.37 – all the disciples praise God for the deeds of power they have seen.

Luke 23.44 – darkness comes over the land from 12-3, and the curtain of the temple is torn.

Luke 24.5 – Jesus is risen.

Luke 24.42-43 – Jesus eats broiled fish.

Luke 24.51 – Jesus is carried up into heaven.

Acts

Acts 2.43 – many signs and wonders were being done by the apostles.

Acts 4.30 – signs and wonders are performed in the name of Jesus.

Acts 6.8 – signs and wonders are done by Stephen.

Acts 8.6-7 – signs, miracles and deliverances occur in Samaria through Philip.

Acts 8.39-40 – Philip is removed by the Spirit from the Gaza road to Azotus.

Acts 9.17-18 – Saul's sight is restored through Ananias.

Acts 9.36-41 – Peter raises Tabitha from the dead in Joppa.

Acts 14.3 – signs and wonders are done in Iconium by Paul and Barnabas.

Acts 15.12 – Paul and Barnabas tell of the signs and wonders done by God among the Gentiles.

Acts 16.26 – an earthquake unfastens the prisoners' chains and releases Paul and Silas from prison.

Acts 19.11-13 – People ware healed and delivered when touched Paul's handkerchiefs.

Acts 20.9-12 – Paul restores Eutychus who dies falling out of a window.

Acts 28.3-6 – Paul is bitten by a poisonous snake without effect.

Prophecy

A spontaneous word spoken for the benefit of others

John

John 1.6-9,15 – John came as a witness to testify to the light

John 1.23 – I am the voice of one crying out in the wilderness, "Make straight the way of the Lord", as the prophet Isaiah said.

John 1.29-36 – John identifies Jesus as the Lamb of God who takes away the sin of the world.

John 1.51 – Jesus says Nathanael will see heaven opened and angels ascending and descending on the Son of Man.

John 2.19 – Jesus offers a sign on demand – 'destroy this temple, and in three days I will raise it up'

John 3.14 – Jesus tells Nicodemus, 'just as Moses lifted up the serpent in the wilderness, so must the Son of Man be lifted up, that whoever believes in him may have eternal life'.

John 3.28-30 – John the Baptist identifies Jesus again as the Messiah, and says 'he must increase, but I must decrease'.

John 4.21,26 – the Samaritan woman says Jesus is a prophet. He says the hour is coming when you will worship the Father neither on this mountain nor in Jerusalem; and identifies himself as the Messiah.

John 5.25-29 – 'the hour is coming when the dead will hear the voice of the Son of God, and those who hear will live.. all who are in their graves will hear his voice and will come out... '

John 6.35-54 – Jesus explains he is the bread of life, and will never drive any away but raise them up on the last day.

John 8.12 – 'I am the light of the world; whoever follows me will never walk in darkness but will have the light of life.'

John 8.21,28 – 'I am going away, and you will search for me, but you will die in your sin. Where I am going, you cannot come...When you have lifted up the Son of Man, then you will realize that I am he'.

John 8.51 – 'whoever keeps my word will never see death'.

John 11.4 – Jesus hears Lazarus is ill, and says this illness does not lead to death, rather it is for God's glory. He stays 2 days longer; Lazarus dies, and is raised.

John 11.51 – Caiaphas, 'being high priest... prophesied that Jesus was about to die for the nation, and not for the nation only, but to gather into one the dispersed children of God'.

John 12.23 –' the hour has come for the Son of Man to be glorified' – like a seed of wheat falling into the ground and bearing much fruit.

John 12.32 – 'I, when I am lifted up from the earth, will draw all people to myself. He said this to indicate the kind of death he was to die'.

John 13.33 – 'I am with you only a little longer. You will look for me; ... where I am going, you cannot come'.

John 13.38 – To Peter: 'you will follow afterward. Before the cock crows, you will have denied me 3 times.'

John 14.3 – 'I go to prepare a place for you... I will come again and will take you to myself, so that where I am, there you may be also'.

John 14.12-14 – 'The one who believes in me will also do the works that I do and, in fact, will do greater works than these, because I am going to my Father. I will do whatever you ask in my name.'

John 14.18-30 – Jesus foretells the coming of the Spirit and warns that the ruler of this world is coming; in a little while they will no longer see him, then they will see him. Because he lives, they also will live.

John 15.18-21 – Jesus warns of persecution ahead for the disciples.

John 15.26 – the promise that the Advocate will come and testify on Jesus' behalf

John 16.2 – 'they will put you out of the synagogues. Indeed, an hour is coming when those who kill you will think that by doing so they are offering worship to God'.

John 16.7-15 – the Advocate will come and guide them; Jesus has many things to say but they could not bear them all now – the Advocate will reveal them

John 16.16-33 – Jesus foretells that he will leave them but return. They will face persecution.

John 21.18 – Jesus tells Peter 'someone else will stretch a belt around you and take you where you do not wish to go' – indicating the kind of death by which he would glorify God.

Luke

Luke 1.13 – Gabriel tells Zechariah his wife will bear a son whom he will name John.

Luke 1.31-33 – Gabriel tells Mary she will bear a son named Jesus, who will reign on the throne of David over the house of Jacob forever.

Luke 1.67 – Zechariah is filled with the Holy Spirit and prophesies about the ministry of John.

Luke 2.26 – It had been revealed to Simeon by the Holy Spirit that he would not see death before he had seen the Messiah.

2.34 – Simeon prophesies over Jesus, and says a sword will pierce Mary's soul too.

Luke 2.38 – a prophet called Anna also prophesies over the child.

Luke 3.2 – the word of God came to John. He prophesies from Isaiah and preaches a baptism of repentance.

Luke 3.16-17 – John announces the coming of one who will baptise with the Holy Spirit and with fire, separate the wheat from the chaff and gather into his granary.

Luke 4.18-21 – Jesus announces that the prophecy of Isaiah has been fulfilled: captives will be released, the blind healed and the oppressed set free.

Luke 11.13 – Jesus says that the Father will give the Holy Spirit to those who ask him.

Luke 11.29 – Jesus warns of judgment on this generation which asks for a sign; it will receive no sign except the sign of Jonah.

Luke 18.31-33 – Jesus says that everything that has written about the Son of Man by the prophets will be accomplished - he will be handed over to the Gentiles, mocked, insulted, spat on, flogged, killed; and will rise on the third day.

Luke 21.6 – Jesus foretells the destruction of the temple.

Luke 21.9-28 – Jesus warns that there will be wars and insurrections, earthquakes, famines, plagues, portents and great signs from heaven. Before that there will be persecution, betrayal, imprisonment and the opportunity to testify. But not a hair of their head will perish; they will gain their souls.

Luke 21.20 – Jesus predicts the siege and destruction of Jerusalem.

Luke 22.16-22 – Jesus tells the disciples he will not eat Passover with them, or drink wine until the kingdom of God comes; and that his body will be given and his blood poured out for the new covenant. And that one of them will betray him.

Luke 22.30 – Jesus tells the disciples they will eat and drink at his table in his kingdom, and sit on thrones judging the 12 tribes of Israel.

Luke 22.34 – Jesus tells Peter the cock will not crow till he has denied him 3 times.

Luke 22.69 – Jesus tells the Council that the Son of Man will be seated at the right hand of the power of God.

Luke 23.28-31 – Jesus tells the weeping women that hard times are coming.

Luke 23.43 – Jesus tells the thief on the cross 'today you will be with me in Paradise'.

Acts

Acts 1.8 – Jesus told them they will receive power when the Holy Spirit comes on them, and witness all over the world.

Acts 11.27-28 – Agabus predicts by the Spirit that there will be a famine; it took place during the reign of Claudius.

Acts 13.1 – there were prophets and teachers in the church at Antioch – Barnabas, Simeon, Lucius, Manaen, Saul.

Acts 13.11 – Paul tells Elymas he will be blinded.

Acts 15.32 – 'Judas and Silas, who were themselves prophets, said much to encourage and strengthen the believers.'

Acts 19.6 – the Ephesians prophesy when they receive the Spirit.

Acts 20.25-30 – Paul tells the Ephesian elders they will not see him again, and warns them that outsiders will come in to attack them, and some from their own group will distort the truth and persuade others to follow them.

Acts 21.9 – the 4 daughters of Philip the evangelist have the gift of prophecy.

Acts 21.10-11 – Agabus prophesies that Paul will be bound and handed over to the Gentiles.

Acts 27.10 – Paul foretells shipwreck and loss of cargo/lives.

Receiving prophetic instructions:

Acts 8.26 – an angel tells Philip to go to the Gaza road.

Acts 9.10-16 – Ananias has a vision, the Lord tells him to go to a certain house, find Saul, and lay hands on him; he will regain his sight and become an instrument to bring the Lord's name before the people.

Acts 10.1-6 – Cornelius has a vision of an angel telling him to send to Joppa for Peter; Peter learns through a vision that he is to go.

Acts 11.5-16 – Peter tells the Jerusalem church how he knew from a vision and a voice that he was to go to Ananias.

Acts 13.2-3 – the Spirit tells Barnabas, Simeon, Manaen, Lucius and Saul that Barnabas and Saul are to be set apart for mission.

Acts 16.6-10 – the Holy Spirit forbids Barnabas and Saul from preaching in Asia and Bithynia, and in a vision Paul hears a man from Macedonia calling him there.

Acts 18.9-11 – the Lord speaks to Paul in a vision, saying that he is to stay in Corinth and not be afraid.

Acts 19.21 – Paul resolves in the Spirit to go to Jerusalem and then to Rome.

Acts 22.6-21 – Paul tells how he first heard the voice of Jesus sending him to Damascus, how Ananias told him what he was to do, how Jesus appeared to him and told him to leave Jerusalem and how he would be sent to the Gentiles.

Acts 23.11 – Paul sees the Lord during the night and is told now he's testified in Jerusalem he is to go to Rome.

Discernment
Knowing whether something is divine, human or demonic in origin

John

John 1.32-34 – 'I saw the Spirit descending from heaven like a dove, and it remained on him. I myself did not know him, but the one who sent me to baptize with water said to me... And I myself have seen.. that this is the Son of God.'

John 1.41 – Andrew says to Simon Peter 'we have found the Messiah'.

John 1.47 – When Jesus saw Nathanael coming he said of him, 'here is truly an Israelite in whom there is no deceit'.

John 1.49 – Nathaniel recognises that Jesus is the Son of God.

John 2.24-25 – Jesus 'knew all people and needed no one to testify about anyone; for he himself knew what was in everyone'.

John 6.64 – 'Jesus knew from the first who were the ones who did not believe, and who was the one that would betray him'.

John 6.70-71 – 'one of you is a devil. He was speaking of Judas son of Simon Iscariot, for he ... was going to betray him'.

John 7.17 – 'Anyone who resolves to do the will of God will know whether the teaching is from God or whether I am speaking on my own'.

John 8.41-47 – Jesus tells the Pharisees the devil is their father, not God. 'Whoever is from God hears the words of God. The reason you do not hear them is that you are not from God'.

John 19.19-22 – Pilate is afraid when he hears Jesus has claimed to be the Son of God. He has an inscription put on the cross, 'Jesus of Nazareth, the King of the Jews'. He refuses to change it: 'What I have written, I have written'.

John 21.7 – John recognises the resurrected Jesus as the Lord.

Luke

Luke 1.41-43 – Elizabeth is filled with the Holy Spirit, and recognises that Mary is the mother of the Lord.

Luke 2.28 – Simeon recognises baby Jesus as the Messiah.

Luke 4.34 – An unclean demon cries out 'What have you to do with us, Jesus of Nazareth?.. I know who you are, the Holy One of God'.

Luke 6.18 – Jesus heals the sick and cures those troubled with unclean spirits.

Luke 7.21 – Jesus has cured many of diseases, plagues and evil spirits.

Luke 11.14 – Jesus casts out a demon from a mute person, who then speaks.

Luke 13.11-13 – Jesus sets free a woman with a spirit that had crippled her for 18 years, saying she has been bound by Satan.

Acts

Acts 1.26 – the disciples choose Matthias by casting lots.

Acts 6.5 – the disciples choose deacons full of faith and the Holy Spirit.

Acts 8.23 – Peter sees that a magician named Simon has the gall of bitterness and the chains of wickedness in his heart.

Acts 13.10 – Paul recognises the devil in Elymas, a false prophet.

Acts 16.18 – Paul recognises the evil spirit in the divining slave girl.

Tongues and their interpretation
Speaking or interpreting foreign or angelic tongues

Acts 2.3-4 – the disciples speak in other languages when the Spirit falls on them at Pentecost. Visiting pilgrims hear these as their own.

Acts 10.46 – the new believers in Caesarea receive the gifts of the Spirit and speak in tongues.

Acts 11.15 – Paul explains that Cornelius and his household had received the gift the believers in Jerusalem first received.

Acts 19.6 – the Ephesians receive the Spirit and speak in tongues and prophesy.

For further reading

There are many books on the ministry of the Holy Spirit today. Here are just a few of those which touch specifically on spiritual gifts. Other works are referred to in the endnotes.

Josephine Bax: *The Good Wine - Spiritual renewal in the Church of England*, CHP 1986

Stanley Burgess (ed): *International Dictionary of Pentecostal & Charismatic Movements*, Zondervan 2003

Mark Cartledge: *Encountering the Spirit*, DLT 2006

Bruce Collins: *Prophesy! A practical guide to developing your prophetic Gift*, New Wine 2000

José Comblin: *The Holy Spirit and Liberation*, Burns & Oates 1989 (1987)

Jack Deere: *Surprised by the Voice of God*, Kingsway 1996

Jack Deere: *The Beginner's Guide to the Gift of Prophecy*, Vine Books 2001

Gordon D Fee: *The First Epistle to the Corinthians*, Eerdmans 1987

Mitch Finley: *The Seven Gifts of the Holy Spirit*, Liguori 2001

Donald Gee: *Concerning Spiritual Gifts*, repr Gospel Publishing House 2007 (first published 1947)

Margery Kempe: *The Book of Margery Kempe*, Penguin 2004

Alison Morgan & John Woolmer: *In His Name: a training course for healing prayer teams*, ReSource 2008

John Owen: *The Spiritual Gifts –(Pneumatologia Book IX)*, Diggory Press 2007

John Owen: *The Holy Spirit – his Gifts and Power*, Kregel Publications 1954

Simon Ponsonby: *God Inside Out – an in-depth study of the Holy Spirit*, Kingsway 2007

David Pytches: *Come Holy Spirit*, Hodder & Stoughton 1995 (fist pub 1985)

ReSource Magazine issue 10: *The Gifts of the Spirit* (www.resource-arm.net)

Mark Stibbe: *Know your Spiritual Gifts,* 2nd edition Zondervan 2004 (1997)

Jean-Jacques Suurmond: *Word and Spirit at Play*, SCM 1994

Anthony Thiselton: *The First Epistle to the Corinthians,* Eerdmans 2000

CR Vaughan: *The Gifts of the Holy Spirit*, Banner of Truth Trust 1984 (1894)

C Peter Wagner: *Discover Your Spiritual Gifts*, revised ed. Regal Books 2005

John Wimber & Kevin Springer: *Power Evangelism*, Hodder 1985

J Rodman Williams: *Renewal Theology*, Zondervan 1996

Keith Warrington: *Jesus the Healer*, PaternosterPress 2000

Tom Wright: *Simply Christian*, SPCK 2006

John Woolmer: *Healing & Deliverance*, Monarch 1999

Other ReSource publications

ReSource publishes a full colour magazine three times a year. Each issue treats a different topic, and contains articles, testimonies, book reviews, poetry and images. Issue 10 is devoted to the Gifts of the Spirit, and includes an article by David Pytches. Issue 7 is on Healing and Deliverance. *ReSource* is edited by Christine Zwart.

In His Name is a practical training course for healing prayer teams by Alison Morgan and John Woolmer. 'Far and away the most balanced, informed, practical guide for church healing teams. The authors have seen much healing - physical, psychological and spiritual, and have the theological and biblical underpinning to ground it. The course is interactive, beautifully written and has been tested over ten years.' - Michael Green.

Season of Renewal is a Lent course by Alison Morgan and Bill Goodman. Combining traditional elements with a fresh approach, it is ideal for groups and churches who want something a little different which will provide a gentle introduction to the work of the Holy Spirit and act as a stimulus for future growth.

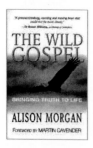

The Wild Gospel takes a personal and challenging look at the ministry of Jesus, the ministry of the Church and the experience of faith today. 'A ground-breaking, exciting and moving book that could not be more timely as the Church looks for fresh ways of speaking God's truth in and to our culture' - Archbishop Rowan Williams

All these and others are available from www.resource-arm.net.

Endnotes

[1] David Hay has suggested that spirituality is a biological phenomenon - *Something There – the biology of the human spirit*, DLT 2006

[2] Simon Ponsonby gives a good description of this process, *God Inside Out*, ch 4 'The Holy Spirit in historical development', Kingsway 2007

[3] Historians complain that in our various great traditions he has been identified with the structures and decisions of the Church, imprisoned in the Word or confined to the sanctuary. See especially J. Comblin, *The Holy Spirit and Liberation*, Burns & Oates 1989; Jean-Jacques Suurmond, *Word and Spirit at Play*, SCM 1994

[4] Raniero Cantalamessa, *The Mystery of God's Word*, Liturgical Press 1994, chapter 6.

[5] Lenin said 'Electricity will replace God. the peasants should pray to it; in any case they will feel its effects long before they feel any effect from on high' – quoted by Philip Yancey, *Prayer*, Hodder 2006

[6] 'Faith and the Public Square', a lecture given at Leicester Cathedral, 22 March 2009.

[7] David Hay, *Something There – the Biology of the Human Spirit*, DLT 2006 ch 1.

[8] See for example the work of Danah Zohar, Frances Vaughan and Mario Beauregard. Writers for the general market include Tony Buzan, *The Power of Spiritual intelligence* (HarperCollins 2001) and Brian Draper, *Spiritual Intelligence – a new way of being* (Lion 2009).

[9] The image of concreting over running water is developed by Tom Wright, *Simply Christian*, SPCK 2006, ch 2.

[10] In his introduction to Jonathan Sacks, *Faith in the future*, DLT 1995 p x.

[11] Rodney Stark, *The Rise of Christianity: a sociologist reconsiders history*, Princeton University Press 1996.

[12] Quoted by D. J. Hall: *The End of Christendom and the Future of Christianity*, Trinity Press International, 1995, p. 18.

[13] *International Dictionary of Pentecostal & Charismatic Movements*, ed Stanley Burgess, Zondervan 2003, p 284.

[14] For a discussion of the spiritual serach of Generation X see Eddie Gibbs and Ian Coffey: *Church next – quantum changes in Christian ministry*, IVP Leicester 2001, ch 5.

[15] Ponsonby 2007 ch 1

[16] See especially John 14-16.

[17] The 'gifts' are described in 1 Corinthians 12-14, the fruit in Galatians 5.

[18] Luke 14

[19] Sulpicius Severus, *Life of St Martin*, ch 26, A Select Library of Nicene and post-Nicene Fathers of the Christian Church, vol 11, New York 1894.

[20] See John Wimber, *Power Evangelism*, Hodder 1985, Mark Stibbe, *Know your Spiritual Gift*, 2nd edition Zondervan 2004, John Woolmer, *Healing & Deliverance*, Monarch 1999, Simon Ponsonby, *God Inside Out*, Kingsway 2007, Mark Cartledge, *Encountering the Spirit*, DLT 2006, Jack Deere, *Surprised by the Voice of God*, Kingsway 1996

[21] *The Book of Margery Kempe*, Penguin 2004, chapters 33 and 40.

[22] From an account by John Howie, in Jack Deere, *Surprised by the Voice of God*, Kingsway 1996, chapter 5. Many of the Scottish Reformers were known for their use of gift of prophecy.

[23] We will explore Jesus's use of the gifts of the Spirit in greater depth in Parts 2 & 3.

[24] John 14.12, 16.7;Luke 24.49; Acts 1.8.

[25] Tom Wright, in a lecture to Fulcrum at St Mary's Islington, April 2005

[26] John Owen, *The Spiritual Gifts (Pneumatologia Book IX)*, Diggory Press 2007, chapter 6.

[27] John Wimber & Kevin Springer: *Power Evangelism*, Hodder 1985, p 44-47.

[28] See Anthony Thiselton, *The First Epistle to the Corinthians*, Eerdmans 2000, p 900.

[29] Augustine's analysis of Spirit as love gift is in his 15 volume work *The Trinity*. See Romans 5.5.

[30] Romans 12, Ephesians 4.Other gifts often cited include hospitality (1 Peter 4.9), missionary (1 Cor 9.19-23), celibacy (1 Cor 7.7-8), intercession (James 5.14-16) and martyrdom (1 Cor 13.3).

[31] The best known comprehensive listing of gifts of the spirit is Peter Wagner's 'Modified Houts' Questionnaire, developed from Dr Richard Houts' 1976 gift discovery programme and now published by the Charles E Fuller Institute. See www.exchristian.net/images/wagner_modified_houts.pdf or C Peter Wagner, *Discover Your Spiritual Gifts*, revised edition Regal Books 2005.

[32] *Dorea*, like dowry, is a word which carries legal undertones.

[33] 1 Corinthians 9.19-23.

[34] See 'Gifts of the Spirit' by JR Michaels in *International Dictionary of Pentecostal & Charismatic Movements*, ed Stanley Burgess, Zondervan 2003; Gordon Fee's *The First Epistle to the Corinthians*, Eerdemans 1987, p 618-19; Anthony Twiselton's *The First Epistle to the Corinthians*, Eerdemans 2000, p 1329.

[35] John Wimber & Kevin Springer: *Power Evangelism – signs and wonders today,* Hodder 1985. See also Deere 96 ch 11

[36] By the Belgian Catholic theologian José Comblin, *The Holy Spirit and Liberation,* Burns & Oates 1989, p. 86.

[37] My colleague John Benson remarks that it is almost as if the Holy Spirit places a 'receptor' in the life of an individual so that the gift can be quickly plugged in and activated by the Spirit when it is needed for ministry.

[38] 1 Corinthians 1.17-2.16.

[39] James 1.5 and 3.13-17.

[40] See Proverbs 1.20-33; 4.5-6; 8.22-31

[41] Deuteronomy 34.9 (Joshua); Genesis 41.38-39 (Joseph); 1 Kings 3.16-28 (Solomon judges wisely, and see his books Proverbs and Ecclesiastes); Isaiah 11.1-3. Daniel is also said to be full of spiritual wisdom (Daniel 2.21-22, 4.6-9). Isaiah 11 is traditionally understood as a description of spiritual gifts.

[42] Mark 2, 3, 7 and 12; John 8; Matthew 13.54.

[43] Luke 21.15; Acts 4 (Peter and John); Acts 6 (Stephen).

[44] Acts 6.1-6;Acts 15.7-21; 2 Peter 3.15. He adds that they are sometimes hard to understand!

[45] We know both much and little about these gnostic philosophies due to their widespread but secret nature. A helpful article is given by the Catholic Encyclopaedia at www.newadvent.org/cathen.

[46] Paul deals with this in chapter 8 and reminds them of it in 12.2.

[47] 13.2. Note how Paul speaks in a single breath of 'understanding mysteries and all knowledge', implying the distinction is not clearcut.

[48] John 4.16-18; 13.11;18.4; 21.4-6.

[49] Acts 5.3; Acts 27.21-26.

[50] 2 Kings 6.8-10.

[51] Mark 11.22-24.

[52] 1 Kings 18.17-40; Daniel 6.23.

[53] Luke 5.20; 7.9; 8.48.

[54] Matt 14.28-31;Acts 15.8-9.

[55] For a more detailed overview of the ministry of healing see the ReSource healing course *In His Name* by Alison Morgan and John Woolmer.

[56] Eg Luke 5.17,6.19, 8.43.

[57] Eg Mark 7 and 9, two people who were both deaf and dumb.

[58] 2 Kings 20.1-11, 2 Kings 5.1-4. For a general statement about healing see Ps 103.3. Many of the psalms talk about inner healing.

[59] Jesus announces his ministry of healing and deliverance in Luke 4, referring to Isaiah 35.5-6 and 61. He sends out the disciples to heal, Matt 10.8. He challenges them to believe in him because of his works, John 10.38.

[60] Gal 4.13, 1 Tim 5.23.

[61] Testimonies to healing can be found in the ReSource healing course *In His Name*, in ReSource magazine and on www.resource-arm.net/onlinearticles.html, as well as in. See also Alpha News at www.uk.alpha.org, or type 'Healing on the Streets' into Google!

[62] Exodus 7.3 ff (plagues), Exodus 14 (Red Sea), Exodus 16 (manna), (1 Kings 17-18 (Elijah), 2 Kings 2-4 (Elisha). John 2 (water into wine), Matt 14 (feeding of the 5000), Luke 8 (storm), Luke 7 (widow's son), John 11 (Lazarus), Luke 8 (Jairus's daughter).

[63] Acts 9 (Tabitha), Acts 20 (Eutychus), Acts 8 (Philip), Acts 6 (Stephen), Acts 16 (earthquake), Acts 28 (snake).

[64] See http://www.heavensfamily.org/ss/daniel_main. Other remarkable examples are given by Mark Stibbe, *Know your Spiritual Gifts*, 2nd ed Zondervan 2004 p98.

[65] Utugi Kamau leads Vanguard Ministries, Nairobi, Kenya. For dry rot see Leviticus 14!

[66] Joel 2.28-30 and Acts 2.17-18; 1 Corinthians 14.3.

[67] FL Godet says a miracle produces an effect in the spiritual domain similar to that produced on the sick man by the 'rise and walk' command pronounced by a person with the gift of healing. Ellicott summarises the purpose of prophetic words as building up, stirring up, cheering up. See J Rodman Williams, *Renewal Theology* vol 2 p 383.

[68] 1 Cor 14.29 (and 1 Thess 5.20-21); Jeremiah 1.12. See also Jeremiah 23 for the distinction between true and false prophecy.

[69] Acts 21.10-14.

[70] John 1; John 11.51-52; Luke 1.67, 2.34, 2.38.

[71] Mark 7.24-30.

[72] Acts 11 and 21 (Agabus), 15 (Judas and Silas), 19 and 21 (the Ephesians and the daughters of Philip).

[73] John 14.26; 15.15-20; 21.18.

[74] Acts 13, 20 and 27.

[75] See CM Robeck, 'Prophecy', in *New International Dictionary of Pentecostal and Charismatic movements*, ed Stanley Burgess, Zondervan 203, pp 1008-09.

[76] In a talk given to the first Fulcrum conference, St Mary's Islington, 2005.

[77] See www.tubestation.org. Tubestation is led by Henry Cavender and Kris Lannen. The Times describes it as 'the thumping heart of cool Cornwall'.

[78] For details and examples see Mark Stibbe, *Know your Spiritual Gifts*, p 132-35.

[79] Ezekiel ch 13, Jeremiah 23.

[80] Acts 13.6-12, 16.16-18, Mark 1.21-27.

[81] Luke 8.43, 13.11; John 9.6-7, Luke 11.14.

[82] John Woolmer, 'The Unseen Battle', ReSource magazine issue 7, *Healing and Deliverance*.

[83] See Ephesians 6.12; Exodus 20.4-5.

[84] John 2.25, 1.47; Matt.16.18.

[85] Hebrews 1.14.

[86] Mark 16.17 – part of the 'longer ending' of Mark held by many scholars to have been added to the gospel at a later date.

[87] 1 Corinthians 12.30 (tongues are not for all), 13.1 (human and angelic tongues). Believers in Caesarea (Acts 10.46) and in Ephesus (Acts 19.6) also speak in tongues when the Spirit comes on them – though it's not clear if they spoke in recognisable languages or not. The two types of tongues are commonly referred to as xenolalia (foreign tongues) and glossolalia (angelic tongues).

[88] 1 Corinthians 14.

[89] Carlyle May has researched glossolalia in many countries and cultures. Tongues occur in mediums (as in the case of the priestesses at Delphi) and in persons suffering from neurological damage and psychiatric disorders as well as in healthy Christians. See the article on tongues by RP Spittler in *New International Dictionary of Pentecostal and Charismatic movements*, ed Stanley Burgess, Zondervan 2003.

[90] 1 Cor 12.30; 1 Cor 14.39.

[84] The Willesden story was told by Revd Mike Clarkson to the Willesden Area Clergy Renewal Group, and has been verified to me by Rev Caz Dunk who was present at the service, which took place in mid 1995. The Tube story was told to Martin Cavender by the Chaplain of RNAS Yeovilton, who knew the captain. Hildegard spoke in tongues; this illustration comes from her *Scivias*, an account of her ecstatic experiences.

[85] In earlier years Mike had offered what he believed was from God to the minister in charge of the service, who took final responsibility for what was given to the congregation.

[86] This ministry is of course exercised under the oversight of the minister of the church and bound by the usual norms concerning confidentiality and disclosure.